Drowning

Andy Palmer

For Laura

CONTENTS

1

In primary school I used to have a survival kit I'd made using the *SAS Survival Guide*. It consisted of:

- Wax-coated matches
- Magnifying glass
- Fishhooks and line
- Beta light
- Snare wire

Now I had another survival kit, a simpler, more effective one. It only had three items:

- Booze
- Fags
- Drugs

It started in secondary school, when puberty hit at thirteen. At my Grandad's, where I went to unwind, I had my first cigarette.

I'd decided to take it and smoke it when I got home. So,

I got one from his pack and put it in my trouser pocket. But on the drive home I made the mistake of holding my leg straight out and as still as possible for fear of damaging it. With me protecting my leg like it was broken, my mum knew I was hiding something.

Looking in the mirror, she said, "What's wrong with your leg?"

I moved my hand over the cigarette in my pocket and shook my head. "I'm fine."

"What's in there?"

"Nothing." I felt my cheeks flush.

We reached home and I thought I'd made it. But she knew. She pulled me to her and pointed. "Show me." I shook my head, so she grabbed my pocket and pulled out the cigarette. She held it in my face.

"Sorry," I said, and looked at the floor.

"This is going straight in the bin," she said, screwing it up in her hand. "Get inside."

I walked into the house with my head down.

The next time, I decided to smoke while *at* my Grandad's, so I wouldn't get caught. The smell on my clothes would be expected.

My Grandad's TV was for news and sport only, except when Fred Dibnah was on. Fred was dressed in his blue overalls, flat cap and glasses with greasy hands leaning on a machine and talking mechanics. He looked exactly like my Grandad had when he still worked.

"He knows his clog iron," said my Grandad, as he walked over to turn the wireless down so he could hear what Fred had to say. I saw the opportunity and slid a cigarette out of his pack.

"Just off to the toilet, Grandad."

He nodded, keeping his eyes fixed on the TV.

I took the cigarette and a lighter with me and, once behind the bathroom door, I lit the cigarette and took a huge drag. I held the smoke in my mouth for a second and then sucked it into my lungs. I felt the scratch in my throat and then I went dizzy and felt like I'd be sick. Saliva gathered at the sides of my tongue and I felt fragile. I let the smoke out and waited. It subsided, so I took another drag, but more slowly. That time it felt okay. The dizziness had gone and I was left with a light head and warm feet. I kept going, watching myself in the mirror sucking the smoke in and letting it flow out through my mouth and nose, until it was finished. Then I threw the butt in the toilet and flushed it away. I splashed water on my face and headed back downstairs.

But the smoking alone didn't cut it, so next came booze.

I knocked on my grandad's door. There was no answer, so I opened it and pushed, but after four inches it stopped on the chain. I heard a shuffling of footsteps inside and then he said, "Who is it?"

"It's me, Grandad. Can I come in?"

He grunted and slipped the chain from the latch.

The living room was dark except for the TV and the glowing tip of his cigarette. The rest of the house was in darkness. He sat on the end of the couch facing the TV and I sat next to him. On the coffee table in front of us were his cigarettes and whisky glass.

"Been at school today?" he said, as he took a drag on his cigarette and let the smoke pour from his nose in two streams like a dragon.

"Yeah," I said, slumping back into the couch.

We both stared at the TV.

"That good, eh?"

I picked up his mug and said, "Do you want a drink?"

"At thirteen, I was up at Walter Frank's doing my apprenticeship," he said.

I looked at him, but he looked forward. He took another drag on his cigarette that was now down to the filter and burning the orange paper. Then he pushed off the glowing tip into the ashtray with the ends of his thumb and forefinger.

"I'll make some tea," I said.

As I walked into the kitchen he said, "Learning a trade would be best if you're not into that academic stuff. You can always fall back on a trade, lad."

I filled the kettle, got a mug for myself and put it next to his. He liked to use the same one for the whole day even though it was orange inside from all the tannic build-up.

As I put tea bags into the mugs, I caught sight of the bottle of scotch on the counter. I picked it up and unscrewed the cap. The smell was hot and spicy, and reminded me of Christmas cake. I took a sip. It was hotter and sharper than I expected. My mouth filled with saliva and my jaw loosened. I rolled it across my tongue before swallowing and hoped that it would stay down. It was like heartburn. Good heartburn that flowed down into your stomach, instead of up. I took another sip and splashed some into my tea. I felt like an adult. I felt stronger.

When my Grandma died the joy was sapped from my grandad and the house. Now he lived in that darkened living room – curtains permanently drawn – sipping whisky and effervescent codeine, smoking endless Craven A cigarettes, and listening to the drone of the wireless. The days of helping him in the garage on his lathe were over. No more model traction engines were to be made. The garden was overgrown. The crabapples were wizened, the loganberries pecked by birds, and the runner bean poles tangled with weeds.

But I liked it there. It was the only place I felt relaxed. Often, we would fall asleep in front of the TV on a Saturday afternoon with the soothing, monotonous sound of the football results being read out – *Millwall one, Nottingham Forest nil; Leyton Orient three, West Bromwich Albion two*. The way the tone of the voice dropped when announcing the lower score lulled me to sleep. Occasionally I was allowed a small can of

Mackeson stout and sometimes a sip of his whisky and codeine.

But I betrayed him.

I stood at his door, my hand poised to knock. I ran over the plan: *sit down and chat, make some tea, and take some money*. It was simple, but terrible.

I knocked, and the light came on in the kitchen.

You don't have to do it.

I heard him cough and shuffle to the door. He opened it on the chain and peered out.

"Oh, it's you. Come in."

I rubbed my sweaty hands on my trousers and followed him through to the living room.

He won't notice a small amount missing.

I perched on the edge of the couch and watched the winding blue smoke rise out of the ashtray.

Just look at how much is there. You don't have to take any.

"I'll put the kettle on," I said.

I walked out of the living room with shaking legs. In the kitchen I filled the kettle and waited until it started to boil, so the noise would cover the sound of me walking to his coat hanging in the hallway. I crept past the door and down the hall. My hands shook as I fumbled with the button on his inside pocket. I had the wallet in my hands.

I stood still and listened. The kettle clicked off. I looked inside and there was a wad of twenties.

He won't notice one gone.

I pulled out a note and stuffed it into my pocket.

This isn't right.

I heard a sound from the living room and jammed the wallet back inside the coat. I could hear the note rustling as I walked back to the kitchen.

I placed the tea down on the table and looked at the TV. My heart was thumping.

Don't act weird or he'll know.

On the news was a girl lying in a hospital bed with tubes in her mouth and arms and a bleeping monitor beside her. "What's happened to her?" I said.

"Drugs. Ecstasy," he said.

I took a sip of my tea and tried to relax. I couldn't look at him. I wanted to leave.

"I don't mind folk having a drink, but drugs," he shook his head, "you can't trust 'em."

I didn't know what to say. I couldn't concentrate. I could feel the money in my pocket. I could hear it. I took another sip of tea. "I've gotta go."

"Okay, lad. I'll see you later."

I felt different walking back down his drive. A cigarette and a sip of whisky didn't feel too bad, but money felt different.

What have I done?

My stomach was tight and my hands still shook. I thought about the booze I could now buy and I felt excited. I'd get drunk and then go to my Grandad's later to stay over. My parents would never know.

After downing a bottle of Thunderbird with a few mates in Spooners Park, I said I'd meet them at seven that night.

"I'm getting my stuff and going to Grandad's," I said, as I ran from the front door and up the stairs.

If I'm quick, she'll never know.

"I've made dinner," my mum said from the bottom of the stairs.

"I'll get something there."

I got the leftover money out of my sock and stuffed it into my pack of fags in front of the cigarettes, and headed downstairs. I got halfway and my mum called from the kitchen, "I'll give you a lift."

I stopped. I couldn't let her get too close. "It's fine, I'll walk."

"Okay."

I listened for her to go back into the kitchen, before carrying on. I laced my trainers and headed for the door.

"Home by ten, remember?"

I froze. She was right behind me. As I reached for the door handle, she said, "What can I smell?"

"Mum, I've gotta go."

There was no way out.

"You've been drinking."

How does she do it?

"Why do you always say that?"

"I'm not stupid. I can smell it from here."

"I had one can of lager."

She came closer and looked right at me. "You've had more than that; your eyes are red."

"I haven't."

"Don't lie to me. You're slurring your words."

It was over. I was caught. I could handle it, as long as she didn't find anything else.

"Where did you get it?"

"Just a friend."

"Have you been smoking as well? Where are they?"

I clung to my bag and turned to go upstairs.

"Bag," she said, and grabbed it from my hands. She started going through the pockets before pulling them from the side.

"Are these your friend's as well?"

There was no way out. *Please don't open the box. Please.* But it was too late. I couldn't watch. I heard the notes being pulled out and I flinched.

"Whose money is this? Have you stolen it?"

I couldn't hide anything. She just knew.

I stared at the floor. There was no way of containing the situation. It was all out there. My stomach tensed and I went cold. I shuffled my feet and said, "I'm sorry."

"Is it your Grandad's?"

I couldn't say it. It was too bad to say out loud. I stared

at her, then at the floor.

Yes, it's Grandad's.

"Right, you're going down there to apologise," she said.

I stood there in the hallway. I couldn't move.

"How dare you steal from your Grandad? From anybody…" She trailed off as she went to get my dad.

A hollow feeling in my stomach was growing with every second we got closer to his house.

This is the worst thing I've ever done. And to the best person I know. How am I going to face him?

"Hi, love. I wasn't expecting—"

"Can we come in?"

He took the chain off the door and we walked into the warmth. He sat down on the couch and my parents and I stood in front of him. I stood a foot behind them, but my mum pushed me forward.

"Tell him what you've done." She looked at me and folded her arms.

My legs were shaking and I couldn't look up at him.

He looked at me as he usually did. As a friend. Like he was happy to see me. But I knew as soon as I told him what I'd done, his face and tone would change. I didn't want it to change, so I just stood there.

"What's up, lad?" he said.

I tried to step back, but my mum's hand was on my back holding me there.

"Spit it out then," my mum said. She reached into her pocket, took out the money and put it on the table. My grandad looked down at it and took a drag of his cigarette. I looked at him, but he didn't look up.

"I took it." I couldn't swallow. I watched the smoke flowing out of his nose and rolling up into the air. We all stood staring down at the money and at my grandad.

"He stole twenty pounds."

He picked the money up and looked at it, before putting

it back on the table. He took a final drag of his cigarette and stubbed it out. He looked at me. His face was relaxed and his eyes were wet. "Why?" he said.

My mum answered. "So he could get drunk. Look at the state of him."

I could feel my stomach rolling and acid creeping up my throat. I wanted to be anywhere else but there. My parents looked at me. My grandad looked at the money on the table.

"What have you got to say?" my dad said.

"Sorry." I felt my cheeks flush and heat prickle my forehead.

"Okay," he said, looking up at me again. He took another cigarette from his pack and struck his lighter.

I wanted him to be angry, but he just shook his head and breathed out the smoke from his lungs.

It was a while before I was allowed to step foot in my Grandad's house again. Once I had a job and my own vehicle, he saw me as more responsible. But things still weren't the same as they used to be.

Now there was no time left to rebuild the relationship.

Everyone would have heard me coming on my raspy motorbike, as I wound through the estate towards my grandad's. As I turned the corner onto his street, his white wrought iron gates stood out against the grey of the tarmac. But something was different. They were gaping open. He always kept them closed. And there were two cars parked outside. My mum and uncle were there. And at that moment, I knew something was wrong.

I drove straight onto his driveway outside the kitchen door and fumbled with the kickstand on my bike. My chest thumped and my hands shook, as I stood in front of the white and blue door. It was ajar, letting a shaft of nicotine-yellow light fall on the step and down onto the driveway. I pushed open the door and was met with the smell of cigarettes and settled dust. Everything looked the same in the kitchen, but it was still and quiet. The door to the living room was shut and behind it were the faint voices of my family talking in hushed tones. I went in.

"Where've you been? We've been trying to find you," my mum said, grabbing my arm and pulling me towards her.

I stared at her flustered face. "What's happened?" I said. Tears were already rolling down my cheeks, but I didn't know why. I didn't even want to think about it.

"He went quietly. He wasn't in pain." She tried to hug me, but I pulled away.

"I want to see him. Where is he?"

"They had to take him. I'm sorry." She took my hand.

"Why did you let them take him?" I pulled my hand from hers and turned to look at everyone else. They were stood, my dad, my uncle, my aunt, in a crescent shape around the couch, staring at where he used to sit. I stared too, at the dent in the couch and the ashtray still full of orange cigarette butts. I looked up and there was a yellow circle staining the ceiling above where he sat. They were all that was left of him.

The room was cold and clinical like a crime scene, lit up by the ceiling light that was never normally on. The wireless and television had been turned off, the smoke cleared out, and someone had tidied up. I felt empty, like a gust of wind had blown through me.

"Did you all see him?" I said.

My aunt pulled me close and hugged me. "We didn't know where you were," she said.

"Why didn't you wait?" I walked out of the room and upstairs. I went into the bathroom and sat on the edge of the bath and lit a cigarette.

I walked around the other rooms like I was looking for clues, but it was all the same as usual. The unused stair lift was still piled with old coats; the brown and orange patterned 70s carpet still ran from the landing, down the stairs and along the hall with a threadbare strip down the centre; the bedrooms were still filled with old boxes; and in my

Grandad's room there were tablet boxes piled high and cigarette butts spilling from ashtrays on his bedside cabinets.

I walked back downstairs and my mum was waiting at the bottom.

"Do you want a cup of tea?" she said.

I ignored her. *What good will tea do?*

Between the living room and dining room was a curtained arch. I walked through it, ignoring the other three. I opened the drinks cabinet and took out a bottle of whisky and some cigarettes, and sat on a dining chair in the bay window and unscrewed the cap.

This was my way of dealing with things; this was my survival kit.

I knocked back three gulps of whisky and lit a cigarette. Now it smelled like he was still here. Now I tasted what he tasted when he was still here. Now my belly felt hot and angry. *He should still be here.* There was no sense to it.

Another gulp.

This was the room we all gathered in for a party when I was six and no one told me what it was for. I was happy to see everyone and ran around in and out of the curtains and under the table while all the adults stood and solemnly ate cheese sandwiches and drank beer and wine. No one wanted to play with me and my mum told me to sit down and be quiet. And in the corner my Grandma was crying.

Another gulp.

They didn't tell me they'd been to a funeral. They didn't tell me it was a sad occasion. I was left to figure it out. And I did. As we left I hugged my Grandma and told her, "It was such a nice party, Grandma, and everyone was here. Everyone but Uncle Kenneth." And my Grandma cried again and bent down to hug me. But they still didn't say anything.

I lit another cigarette and pulled hard on it.

"Are you okay in there?" My mum poked her head through the heavy curtains.

I looked at her and took a long gulp from the bottle.

"If you need anything, we're just…" She closed the curtains.

How do you make sense of all this?

It seemed a lifetime ago since I baked coffee kisses and raspberry buns with my Grandma, stirring the mixture in a bowl while stretching on a stool to reach. I could picture her curls popping out from underneath her green woolly hat, her round face and short, slightly bent stature. But I couldn't hear her voice. That was lost long ago.

When she was in the hospital bed in the living room, I'd run in whipping through the curtain and jump into bed with her. Then, I'd reach under the bed and pull out the box with the squidgy blob in it and let it flop into my hands, dropping it from one to the other, and then I'd squish it like a stress ball. I once asked if I could keep it and my Grandma said yes, but my mum said no.

No one told me anything that time, either.

That day I went running through the curtains shouting, "Grandma, Grandma," looking for her bed, but it was gone and so was she.

I was eight.

I drank deeply from the bottle again, letting it burn down my oesophagus. I sucked on the cigarette and drew the smoke into my lungs and held it there to get the most I could out of it. This is how I coped with feeling too much. This is how I survived the feelings that threatened to take over.

I drank again. The bottle was half empty. I walked out of the dining room back to where the four of them were sat drinking tea on his couch. In his seat.

"I'm going," I said.

"Come and sit down with us," my mum said, but I knew she wouldn't stop me.

"I'm fine."

I walked out of the door and into the dark. I started my bike and sat on it in the driveway and finished my cigarette.

My mum came to the door. "Come back inside. We'll talk."

"It's too late."

She stood in the doorway watching me. I turned off the engine and got off. When she turned to go inside, I walked out of the driveway and down the street. I started running, down one street then the next. Then down the ginnel, over the dike and out into the football field.

I didn't know where to go, so I followed my usual route home. My hair was wet with November drizzle and my hand still gripped the bottle. I could feel tears welling in my eyes. To my left was the cemetery and I walked into it.

It seemed like the thing to do.

I found my Grandma's grave, sat down and lit a cigarette. I took a long drink from the bottle and let the tears roll off my chin.

2

Secondary school was hell from day one. And now I was getting thrown out.

That morning before catching the bus to school, I went into the supermarket in the village and stole some beer. I walked to the booze aisle, checked no one was around, lifted a four pack of Budweiser into my rucksack, threw it on my back and walked out. I already had a few cigarettes I'd taken from my Grandad's, so I was all set to meet the lads in the basement at lunch break.

The sound of my shoes slapping the marble steps echoed up the stairwell and within the iron banister. It was three flights down to the basement and the dust became thicker with each step. It was dark inside, but I knew they'd be in the far left corner next to the door that led to the courtyard.

"Did you get the beer?" Steve said.

I didn't answer. I smiled, unzipped my bag and lifted the four pack out onto the stone floor.

"Nice one," Chris said, "let's crack 'em open."

I passed them around and we opened them together.

"Woah!" we said, as the shaken cans frothed over us. We

tipped our heads back and gulped them down, so as not to lose too much.

"Who wants a fag?" I said, pulling three cigarettes from the side pocket.

Steve put his hand up. "No, mate."

"Spark one up, and I'll have half," Chris said.

We shared the last can and finished the cigarette. I found an old grate and dropped the evidence down the hole.

"Come on, let's get back," Steve said.

Steve and Chris ran through the basement and back up the stairs, while I stayed behind to smoke another cigarette.

That afternoon in German class, barely minutes after the usual exchange of, "Guten Morgen Klasse," and our reply of, "Guten Morgen Herr Rowland," I got thrown out and told to stand by the door.

As I stood there, the headmaster, Mr Bavister, walked by. He stood in front of me with his hands on his hips and sighed. "Again?" he said, and nodded towards his office. "Get in there and wait for me."

The next day, my parents and I were summoned for a meeting. We arrived at the school and headed to Barmy Bavvy's office. He was stood in his unassuming uniform of brown corduroy trousers, brown shoes, woolly jumper, and glasses.

"We've had enough. We can't cope with him anymore," he said, as he paced the carpet in front of us.

"What's he done now?" my mum said. She was sat upright with both hands on her lap holding her handbag.

"What's he done? What hasn't he done? He's been a menace since he started." His face was red and he spoke through his teeth. His side-parted grey hair flapped over his left eye every time he spun round.

My mum stood up. "We didn't come here to be shouted at, so let's sit down and talk about it."

"Sit down? Why don't you control your child? He's got

behaviour issues and needs counselling and we're not equipped for that," he said, pointing at the three of us. Whenever I got thrown out of lessons he'd jab that big index finger into my chest over and over again, shouting, "Why can you not be-have your-self in les-sons?" with a sharp dig on every syllable.

"Counselling? He's fifteen. I'm glad we took Hannah out when we did," my dad said.

"Yes, after all the work we put into them you took the well behaved one out and left us with the idiot!"

"Just get to the point or we're leaving."

He stiffened and said, "Your son's bringing alcohol and cigarettes into school and getting other pupils involved."

My parents looked at each other and said, "How was he caught?"

"I smelled smoke on his clothes yesterday and I've heard rumours about the basement."

"So this is a rumour?"

"It's enough. This is a Christian school and we expect Christian behaviour."

In a school of eighty pupils and a year group of twelve, it was hard to keep anything hidden. That's why I spent most of my time in the calm of the basement or in the toilets. They were the only places I didn't feel watched and scrutinised.

"After a litany of incidents these last few of years, we've had enough," Barmy Bavvy continued and listed them on his fingers. "The destruction of Mr Rowland's laptop, pouring glue into the hair of another pupil, swearing at a member of staff, and…" he looked towards the window, "the inappropriate carrying on with Heidi in the back of Miss Turner's Mini Metro on the way home from the theatre. And now this." He joined his arms around his back and turned towards us. "He has to go."

And that was it. I was out.

Back home my dad was silent. He sat in his chair and tapped

his fingers on the arm. My mum didn't say anything either, but she slammed the door shut and went into the kitchen. We could hear cupboards being flung open and pans banged. The mood was tense. She stormed back into the living room and looked at me. Her face was red and puffy. "Just go to your room. I don't want to see you till dinner."

I dumped my bag in the hall and went upstairs.

I welcomed the time on my own. I would only get stared at and shouted at downstairs. I went up into my room and lay on the bed. My bedroom was the box room at the front of the house with a square window facing the street. I often sat on the end of the bed and watched the neighbours walk up and down to their homes. We lived on Common Lane in a brick semi on a street of brick semis. It felt common and boring and normal. I felt common and normal too, and bored.

I picked up my asthma inhaler and took two puffs for my wheezy chest. It tasted awful, but worked. I noticed that the feel of it was like sucking the smoke from a cigarette into my lungs, so I took another two puffs and held them. I liked the feeling of my lungs being full. I thought about school and what had gone on. I felt like I'd lost something, but I felt relieved too.

I decided that I didn't fit in there and they didn't want me, either. I took six puffs on the inhaler and held it. As I let it out, a cold humming sensation went down through my back, from my shoulders to my heels, and started to tingle. I closed my eyes and concentrated on it. My heart was beating faster, my head felt light and a sound in my ears went *zeezoo zeezoo zeezoo zeezoo*.

It wore off in thirty seconds, so again I puffed six times, then six times, then six times, then six times until I was out of breath. The feeling increased and I felt squashed into the bed. I listened to the *zeezoo zeezoo zeezoo* in my ears and tried to lose myself in the sensations until I fell asleep.

I had no choice but to go to my local school after being expelled. Life was not going to be any better at Royston Comp, even though I only had to stick it out for a year.

In the first lesson on the first day, I saw that I was sat two rows in front of Robbo. At primary school he tripped me every lunchtime football match, kicked me in the balls when I told the teacher that he was distracting me, and coined the nickname, *palmtree-pyramid-perfume-Palmer*, that got me laughed at every day.

I already felt so nervous I was scared to look around at the thirty unfamiliar faces sat in rows surrounding me. It was a long way from the dozen I was used to in a warm, carpeted room where we all sat facing one another in a circle.

Then my heart dropped as Robbo got out of his seat and started walking to the front. As he passed me, he walked slower and pushed the books off my desk. The sound alerted the teacher.

"Can I help you, Robert?" said Miss Evans.

"Sharpening my pencil, Miss."

She nodded.

He stood next to her desk and stared at me as he sharpened his pencil. His eyebrows were dark and met in the middle. They raised as he smiled at me. He ground the pencil over and over again, not moving his eyes from mine. As he walked back he leaned over me and said, "You're dead after this lesson," and jabbed the point of the pencil into my hand.

I didn't get chance to ask why, but there didn't need to be a reason. I stared down at the sums I was meant to be doing and could feel his eyes behind me. The numbers and lines on the page swam and I could make no sense of them. *How am I going to get out of this?* I thought.

As the bell rang, I got up, filled my bag and squeezed into the crowd near the door, trying to get out before Robbo came. But it was no use. He dived into the crowd, jumped on my back and dragged me onto the dusty ground. He didn't speak as he screwed his fists into the back of my jumper and tried to slam my face into the wooden floor.

I couldn't speak or move. The best I could manage was to cushion my face with my hands. I could hear the teacher shouting, "Get off him. Someone get Mr Davies."

And then a deep voice said, "Get off 'im you prick," and one of the lads who was a foot taller than everyone else dragged Robbo off me. It was a guy I'd been friends with at primary school, but hadn't seen since.

As the classroom cleared, I got up off the floor and brushed myself down. Miss Evans looked at me and smiled. "Better get off to your next class," she said.

A week or two went by and I got used to the teeming corridors and the draughty wooden buildings of the comp. I liked the anonymity of being one pupil in a crowd of hundreds all looking the same. I'd started to think of what I'd do after school and I thought I'd found it one careers session.

"Okay everyone, come and choose a career file you're interested in." She stood in front of a table filled with blue folders and I felt excited for the first time since arriving. I went to the table and picked up a folder for the Police and headed to a desk near the window. We were on the top floor of the library and the windows looked out over the playing fields. I watched as a PE class threw javelins down the field, the sun glinting off the tips as they flew through the air and descended into the grass.

I was so absorbed I didn't notice Robbo stood behind me. "You done with that?" he said.

"Only just got it." I held it tight.

He yanked it out of my hands. "Whatever." Then smiled and his thick black eyebrows joined above his nose.

There was nothing I could do, so I just sat there. I thought I'd just pretend to be reading until the lesson ended, then leave. But then the teacher came and said, "Where's your folder?" And I had no answer. "What's going on?"

"Someone took it." As soon as the words left my mouth, I knew it was a mistake.

"Who?"

I didn't answer. I stared out of the window and towards the street I lived on and wished I was at home, safe in my room.

She looked round the room. "Who's got the Police folder? Come on, speak up."

No one said anything, so she walked around looking at the folders on everyone's desk until she got to Robbo.

"Thank you," she said, as she scooped it up and brought it back to me. She didn't know what she'd done, but I could feel his eyes on me. I knew there was nothing I could say to deter him.

When the bell went, I hurried down the stairs and checked over my shoulder, but couldn't see him anywhere. I signed out of the library and walked toward the door. I turned and looked up the stairs and he wasn't among the rest of the class filtering down. I was free. I zipped up my coat and put my bag on my back. I pushed the door, but then felt a thud from behind.

The door crashed open and I flew onto the ground face down and hit my head on the concrete slabs. I pulled my arms up and shielded myself. I daren't look to see what was coming next, so just covered my face and cowered. I could hear footsteps and voices all around me. I waited for it. But nothing came. When I opened my eyes, he was gone and everyone else carried on like nothing had happened.

Back at home, I walked into the back garden, hid behind the garage and cried. I felt totally powerless. I wanted to escape from everyone and everything. I'd gone from one school where I couldn't breathe without drawing attention, to one where I went unnoticed even when being bullied. I didn't belong anywhere, but I couldn't get away.

I wiped my eyes and went into the house. No one would be home for a couple of hours, so I went and got my inhaler.

It was nearly empty, so I grabbed a can of deodorant, wrapped a towel around the top and sprayed it into my mouth breathing in the fumes. It worked, and I got the same floating feeling I did with the inhaler. But after a while I got the nasty taste of the fragrance, which made my mouth dry.

I wish my parents drank, I thought. Then I hit on an idea. My dad used strong painkillers for his back and I was sure I knew where he hid them. Maybe they would get me high. I rifled through his bedside cabinet and found them. They were codeine phosphate and I thought they were probably similar to what my Grandad had. I read the leaflet from the box and it listed euphoria and drowsiness as side effects and cautioned against driving when taking them. It sounded good to me, so I swallowed two. I sat on the couch in the living room and read. I started to feel much more content and comfortable and more settled. I read until I felt tired and then slid down and rested my head on a cushion. I wanted more, but felt sick and sleepy, so just lay there staring at the swirly patterned Artex on the ceiling. *I wouldn't mind feeling like this all the time.*

I didn't bother with maths or careers after that, so managed to avoid Robbo.

Around the smokers' corner, where I often nipped through the hedge to skive, I met Danny. He was in the year below, but seemed really cool.

"Save us twos on that, man?" he said.

"Eh?"

"Half your fag."

I nodded. It seemed like the thing people did at the comp, so I didn't want to be weird. "I'm Andy."

"Danny." He nodded at me and spat against the wall. He picked up a stone and threw it over the hedge. He seemed way cooler than me with his hair in curtains and a pair of Kickers boots.

I passed him the half cigarette.

He cupped it in his hand and took a long drag. "Can't be arsed today. Wanna come to mine for a bong?"

We swung our bags on our backs and squeezed through the hedge and around the back of the swimming baths. He only lived round the corner from mine, so we were there in no time.

We walked up to his house and round into his back garden towards the shed. He reached under and pulled out a key and opened the door.

"Put fag in and I'll give you two bongs," he said.

I nodded. "Will I be wasted?"

He laughed and pulled a bucket of water into the centre of the floor. "It's only a bit of pot, man."

I was excited. I passed him a cigarette and he squeezed the tobacco into a bowl made from the bottom of a pop bottle and burnt little pieces of pot and sprinkled them in.

"Hold this." He pushed the remainder of the pop bottle into the water, so that the chamber was submerged with the top sticking out. Then he fashioned a lid from tin foil and poked holes in it with a needle.

"What's it feel like?" I said, my legs shaking. It was the first real drug I'd ever had.

"Awesome, man. You'll love it." He took a pinch of the mixture from the bowl and filled the foil cap. Then he struck the lighter and burnt the mixture while pulling the bottle up from the water. The chamber filled with thick smoke – a whole two litres of it – and my stomach became jittery.

"I'll have this one and you can go next." Danny unscrewed the cap and put his palm over the top to stop the smoke leaking out. Then he placed his mouth over it and pushed his head down, sucking the entire bottle of smoke into his lungs. He sat holding his breath for a long time before releasing the smoke with a huge breath.

His eyes were red and eyelids heavy. He smiled and ran his hand through his dark hair. "Ready for yours?"

He went through the ritual again and held his hand over

the bottle of smoke and nodded for me to come forward and take it. I locked my lips around the top and pushed down towards the water. My lungs felt like they were full with half of the smoke, but I kept going until it was all gone. A fire burned in my chest. I knelt on the ground, closed my eyes and held it for as long as I could before letting it pour out.

"Nice one, man," Danny said.

I felt heavy and my eyelids slid down over my eyes. My whole body felt fuzzy and warm.

"You look proper stoned. Want another?" he said, as he pulled the bottle up.

I shook my head and went to speak, but it felt like too much hassle, so I closed my mouth and smiled and leant back.

In Danny's house we drank the best tasting orange squash and ate the most delicious biscuits I'd ever had in my life. We listened to an album by a new band that was all guitars and northern accents, singing about champagne supernovas and wonderwalls. And we cracked up as we joined in on one of the croaky choruses singing *'where were you while we were getting high?'* before rolling on the floor in stomach churning giggles.

It was a Saturday night and on Saturdays everyone went to the park and got pissed and stoned. That's just what you did. So I'd planned to meet Danny down near the crown green bowling area at six. He was going to bring some special brew he'd nicked off his dad and I was going to bring some codeine off mine. But when I went to get some there weren't enough in the pack for my dad not to notice, so I went searching for something else. I remembered that we kept a key for the next door neighbour's house for emergencies, so I checked that they were out and let myself in.

I walked down the hall and into the living room. The first thing I noticed was the booze cabinet, so I went over and had a look through it – Pernod, ginger wine, navy rum – nothing looked good, but I took a gulp of the rum and kept going. In the kitchen on a high shelf was a basket full of medication. After a rummage, I found a bottle of 100 diazepam and shoved them in my pocket. I knew what type of stuff to look for, as my mum had a drug reference book on the shelf at home and I'd had a look through it.

The park was right in the centre of the village off one of the main roads and had large gates at the entrance and a tree-lined driveway down into it. On the right were the rose gardens and on the left the cricket pitch and bowling green. We always met by the bowling green on the covered benches. They were comfortable, dry and sheltered.

I walked towards Danny. "Hi mate, how's things?"

"Buzzing, man. You get the pills?"

I passed him the bottle.

"Woah, diazzies." His eyes lit up. "Nice one, man."

"Get the beer?" I said, and he lifted a four pack from under the bench.

He looked over the bottle. "Where they from?"

"Next door neighbours'."

"They not gonna miss 'em?"

"Nar, been there for ages. Don't think they take 'em anymore."

He nodded and twisted the cap off. We took one each and gulped it down with the beer and waited. We shared a cigarette and looked out over the neatly trimmed grass on the green.

"They don't do owt," Danny said.

I shrugged. "Let's do more." I tipped out half a dozen into his palm and the same into mine. We chewed them, drained our cans and then went to lie down on the grass.

I stared at the dusk sky and watched the clouds move.

"Can you feel owt yet?" Danny said.

"Legs feel a bit tingly, but nowt else."

"More?" Danny said.

I popped open the tub and we chewed a few more. It wasn't long until I started to feel something.

"I don't feel right, Danny. I feel like a big, wobbly blancmange melting onto the grass."

"Don't talk about food, man. I'm gonna throw up."

And with that Danny rolled over onto his front, pushed himself up and vomited onto the grass. I couldn't see that and not feel a twinge in my stomach so I tried to get up and failed, falling onto my arm and banging my head.

Danny laughed, "What you doing, you knob?" and came and pulled me up. We swayed with our arms over one another's shoulders toward the railings around the edge of the park.

"Mate, I'm messed up," I said, letting my head loll forward so that all I could see were the dark green leaves and pink flowers of the rhododendrons.

"I know, man, feel worse than when I whitey."

We stood holding the railings and threw up into the bushes, then crawled back onto the grass and lay there.

A couple of hours later, we'd regained control of our stomachs and were feeling good after finishing the beer and having a few joints with the other lads. I was sat on the bench smoking when a girl I didn't know came and sat down.

"Wanna drink?" she said and offered me a bottle of purple liquid. I took a sip. It was really sweet after the beer.

"What's that?" I said, screwing up my face.

"Mad Dog."

I shook my head, "It's awful."

She laughed and said, "Better than beer," and took a drink.

I passed her half my cigarette. I was just thinking of something else to talk about when my heart sank. Robbo was swaying towards me. *What's he doing down here?* I got up to walk away, but he came and stood right in front of me.

"You trying to get off with my bird?" He spoke through clenched teeth.

I tried to speak, but could only shake my head.

"Just leave it, Rob," she said.

He threw his empty cider bottle into the hedge. "Get away from her."

"I just—" But before I could explain, he'd hit me.

It was the first time I'd been punched in the face and it felt nothing like I imagined. I didn't have any pain. It felt like I'd been hit with a blow-up toy, but I was numb and my sight was blurred. I pulled myself up off the bench and tried to get away, but his face was in front of me – pale skin, black hair, heavy eyebrows – split into three and mouthing inaudible words.

Then I felt another blow. Again, there was no pain. It was like an intense gust of wind had knocked me, but no pain. This time I fell to the floor. I was awkward like a drunk trying to stand. I didn't know which way was up. I struggled to my feet and stumbled towards the railings. I spun round to see my attacker coming towards me, so I hobbled away as quickly as I could.

He shouted, "Where you off?" as I passed him and he tried to trip me, but I managed not to fall and just kept moving towards the gates of the park.

Someone shouted, "Leave him, he's had enough." But that was it. No one came to help me. None of my friends. Not even Danny.

I had to walk out of the park alone, wiping blood out of my eyes so that I could see. I felt something in my mouth and reached in to get it. It was half a tooth. I moved my tongue through my mouth and felt the shear edge of the broken front tooth. Then I remembered the glint of a ring as his fist came towards my face. I just wanted to feel safe at that moment and to be away from all harm. I wanted my parents and to be at home. I wanted to get Robbo back. I wanted to kill him. I didn't understand why he wanted to hurt me.

I had to think of something to tell my parents. The truth was too embarrassing to admit, even to them. Maybe I could tell them I fell while walking on a wall and landed facedown onto the edge. But they wouldn't buy that. I put my hands in my pockets and noticed I still had the pills. I popped open the bottle and started to chew them. I lit a cigarette and pulled hard. My face hurt, but I was fine. I kept taking the pills until the pain was unnoticeable. I kept smoking until I felt calm.

3

The muffled sound of ten praying adults in the living room below comforted me as a child and helped me sleep. When I was nine I gladly said a prayer with my Sunday school teacher to follow Jesus. A couple of years later, dressed in a white gown, I was dunked in the baptismal pool by the pastor and raised from the water to the sound of Newton's Amazing Grace. But I still had to go through my dangers, toils and snares.

And this wretch was yet to be saved.

Friday nights were Youth Night. If you were eleven or above and part of Bethel Church, you went whether you liked it or not. Me and Jonny were no exception and we met there an hour early every week.

"You get owt from your grandad's, mate?" Jonny said, his eyes wide.

I put my hand up for him to be quiet and nodded. I gestured with my head towards the other side of the street from the church.

"Behind the…?" He flicked his eyes to the side and smiled.

"Let's go," I said, and headed to the back of the Co-op.

We crossed over the road from the church and walked up the embankment between the mechanic's garage and the big house. The track led us behind the supermarket where there was an alleyway hidden between the back of the building and a rock face. I had a hiding place directly in the rock, like a small cave covered by branches and leaves.

"What's that?"

"Diamond White, proper strong cider," I said, pulling it from the wall. "We'll feel this." I passed Jonny a can and we cracked them open.

He gulped a few times and then screwed up his face. "Tastes horrible mate, wish we had some blackcurrant to put in."

"A fag'll help." I took out a couple of Craven A.

"I'm not smoking. I hate it."

I shrugged and lit one. After each gulp I took a drag and it stopped me heaving.

Jonny kept gulping and wincing.

"You ever nick money?" Jonny said.

I shook my head.

He lowered his voice, even though there was no one near, "I grab a handful of quids from the till whenever I go in Mum and Dad's shop. Proper easy." He ran his hand through his side-parted hair.

"You get much?" I said.

"Enough for all these." He pulled out packet after packet of chewing gum. "They'll sort our breath out."

"Nice one."

We finished the cans and stuffed our mouths with Wrigley's Spearmint gum until we couldn't speak, then went back to church.

On the way in, Michael saw us and came over. "Hi guys, how's things?"

"Mmm, hmm," we said, around the lumps of chewing gum.

29

He sniffed the air after we'd hurried past him.

"I can smell smoke," he said, "come here." We walked back over to him, but stayed a couple of feet away. He leaned in and sniffed the front of our tops. "Smells really strong on you, Andy."

I panicked and spat out my gum. "Some lads outside the Co-op were smoking."

"They blew it on us," Jonny said.

He kept looking at us for a bit, like he wasn't sure what to do. Then he said, "You need to keep away from people like that."

In the meeting, Michael did his usual preach, staring at us with his intense eyes and shouting with one arm raised and his finger pointed towards us all.

'The world wants you to do things to please yourself. They say, "If it feels good, do it," but that's not what God wants for you. The world wants you to smoke, drink, do drugs and sleep around, but God doesn't want you to have fun, he wants you to do what he says instead.'

Or something like that. It was always the same preach, us versus the world, but we knew Michael had never been in 'the world' and didn't realise that all those things sounded good to us. He was only in his mid-twenties and had worked for the church since leaving Bible College. This was our main experience of church other than Sunday mornings when our parents dragged us there in our Sunday best. That and the week away at camp every summer.

Camp was always held at some boarding school and this year we were at one near Robin Hood's Bay. A really nice old place, but I didn't really care about that. Everything was possible at camp if you kept under the radar and I always came prepared with cigarettes and booze.

One of the highlights of camp was a day trip to the coast

and this year we were off to Scarborough. Me and Jonny walked to the back of the coach and sat on the rear seats. We were the only ones at the back except another guy we didn't recognise. He had short dreadlocks tied with coloured elastic bands and wore a black T-shirt that read *Spliff in Comfort* in the style of *Southern Comfort*.

"Nice shirt," I said.

"Thanks. I'm Rick." He leant back and ran his hand over the twisted locks of hair.

I looked at his shirt again and the dreadlocks and bangles on his wrists and decided he was like us, but cooler. "You into that?" I said, and nodded at his T-shirt.

He laughed and said, "Maybe, what about you?"

Jonny looked at me and we smiled. "We're up for anything."

Rick lowered his voice and gestured for us to come closer, "Wanna get some poppers?"

We nodded, but I knew neither of us had a clue what poppers were.

He looked back at us with a side smile. "Sweet, we'll hang out then."

As soon as the coach pulled up we were all out of our seats and heading towards the front as Michael shouted, "Right everyone, be back at this exact spot no later than three or the coach will leave without you." We barged out of the doors and headed to the promenade. We walked past the arcades with their electronic sounds, past the burger kiosks with the smell of fried onions, and took a left by the rock shop where bags of pink candyfloss blew in the wind. Then we raced up the concrete steps beside the funicular and arrived at the top next to the Grand Hotel and set off into the town.

"Where we off first?" Jonny said.

"I'm gasping for a fag," said Rick, striding ahead.

We followed him through the streets passing all the usual town centre shops like Boots, WH Smiths and Marks &

Spencer and looked for a suitable hiding place. We had to be careful, as we didn't want to get spotted by anyone. We came to a supermarket and hid behind it. We sat on wooden pallets facing each other and I got a pack of Craven A out.

I held the box towards them.

"Sweet," Rick said, and took one.

Jonny looked away.

"Come on, live a little," Rick said, and passed one to Jonny.

He shook his head.

We shrugged and lit them. We leant back on the wall and relaxed. Rick blew smoke rings.

Jonny sat staring off into the distance, picking up small stones and throwing them into a bush. "I'm not sure about poppers. I don't wanna take any drugs," he said.

Rick sat up. "They're not drugs. You can't buy drugs in a shop."

"I'd rather get some booze," Jonny said.

"Alright, we will," Rick said. "I can get served."

We counted up the money we had and put it in between us.

"Plenty for some beers *and* some poppers," said Rick.

"Diamond White?" I said.

"I'm not drinking that crap," Johnny said.

"Blastaways?" said Rick, "Castaway mixed with Diamond White. Tastes way better and gets you hammered."

Jonny looked at me and I nodded. He looked at Rick and shrugged.

"Sorted, I'm going in."

In under an hour we had polished off a dozen Castaways and a dozen Diamond White.

Jonny said, "What happens when you take poppers?

"Thought you didn't want any?" I said.

Rick shrugged. "Makes you feel warm and happy. Only lasts a few seconds."

Jonny thought for a second. "Screw it, let's get some."

"Good lad," I said.

According to Rick, joke shops were the best place for poppers, so we went in the first one we saw and Jonny walked straight up to the counter and said, "Got any poppers?" at the top of his voice.

The guy stared at him for a second and said, "No, piss off."

So we decided Rick should do the buying again. We waited outside keeping watch as he went in to the next shop. He came out clutching three small bottles of Liquid Gold and handed us one each. I rolled it in my hand and read the label, which said *room odouriser, not to be inhaled directly from the bottle.* I shoved it into my pocket as fast as I could and checked there was no one around we knew. My heart was beating faster with anticipation and I said, "Let's find somewhere to go," and we set off along the winding street down towards the promenade.

Rick pulled us into an alleyway between a shop selling rock and one selling tacky souvenirs. We tore the gold plastic from the top of the bottles and unscrewed them. Facing each other we watched Rick put the bottle under one nostril, a finger on the other and take a long sniff up. His face went red and he spaced out for a few seconds, and then smiled and leant back. We followed him, doing exactly the same. I breathed out and the rush went through my body like static, my heart thumped and head was a cotton wool bud.

"Good innit?" I said, feeling warm, fuzzy and on fire. We laughed together and then all took another big sniff and leant back against the grimy brick wall of the alley.

I'd never used poppers before, but they were something new to escape with and feel with, so I had my nose stuck into the bottle for the rest of the day, just like Jonny and Rick. But by the time we got back on the coach our heads were pounding. We sat right at the back again and nursed them. We didn't speak for a while. I looked out of the window as we drove up the winding road and watched Scarborough slip away behind us.

When I was nine we went to Scarborough on a Sunday School trip. We played games on the coach like the Bible quiz and 'who can see the sea first'. I got the most Bible questions right and won a Mars bar. Then we played more games on the beach and had a packed lunch. I saved my chocolate until the return journey and ate it while everyone else ate their rock and candy floss. I always sat as near to the front as possible, so that I could see when we got near the coast. Back then, the sky was blue, the beach was yellow and everyone was happy.

"I feel sick," I said.

"Worst hangover ever," said Jonny.

Rick laughed. "It's not that bad. Want a pick 'n' mix?" He held out a bag, but we shook our heads.

A young lad was staring at us between the seats in front. Rick leant forward with the bag. "Want one, mate?" The lad took one and turned back around.

Both Jonny and me were sat with our heads in our hands, but Rick was fine. "You're such lightweights," he said, and pulled out his Liquid Gold and started sniffing again. "Hair of the dog?" he laughed.

Back at the camp, I was wandering through the courtyard when I heard a familiar voice shout: "Andy Palmer, get here now!" It was Michael. My heart sank.

"What?"

"Come with me."

"What have I done?" *There's no way he can know what we've been up to in Scarborough.*

He didn't answer me, but kept walking at pace towards the main building, which the leaders had made into their headquarters. He led me into a small sitting room where Jonny and Rick sat with their heads bowed, watched over by two leaders. He gestured for me to sit down next to them. Then for a few moments they just stared at us in silence.

"Have you got some as well?" Michael said.

"Got some what?" I said. Sweat started to bead on my back and roll down it.

"Don't play stupid with me, you know what I'm talking about." His hands were on his hips and his eyebrows were up as high as they could go.

Is it the cigarettes or the poppers? I didn't want to guess and get us in more trouble, so I shrugged.

He turned away shaking his head and paced, before saying, "This isn't a joke. I'm just about to call the police."

We all looked up at him. He had our full attention.

"The poppers," Jonny said, without looking at me.

I took the small bottle out of my pocket and held it out. My legs started to shake.

"What happened on the coach?" Michael said.

We looked at one another and then at Michael. "Nothing," we said.

"Who've you given these to?"

"No one."

Michael was clenching and unclenching his fists while staring at us. "I've got a twelve-year-old kid upstairs who says you've spiked him with a sweet."

"It was just a sweet," Rick said. "Maybe he got a whiff of the poppers."

Michael thought for a moment. "Get back to your dorms and don't tell anyone about this. I'll speak to you after dinner."

I had a corrosive feeling in my stomach and couldn't eat. It got worse until Michael came to get us. We were taken back to the room and made to sit down.

"Right, I've spoken to the boy's mother and she doesn't want the Police involved. But guys, I've gotta say, I'm really disappointed in you."

We all had our heads bowed, expecting to be sent home.

"Washing up duty and litter picking all week. And if I hear of anything else, you're going home."

It wasn't just me and Jonny making Michael's life a misery. Lee, one of the older guys in Youth, bought a house and started to have parties and he invited a lot of the younger youth.

It was at one of these parties that I met Lena.

The house and garden were full of people milling around. The sound of loud dance music ignited the air with an electric pulse, sending tremors through the rooms.

I'm blue, dab a dee, dab a die
Da ba dee, dab a die
Da ba dee, dab a die…

I was in the kitchen getting a drink when a girl I didn't know introduced herself.

"I'm Lena," she said, standing so close to me I could smell her perfume.

"Andy." I smiled and held her eyes with mine. Her hair was pinned up, showing her soft jawline and heart shaped face.

"I like your shirt," she said, and put her hand on my chest.

"D'you want a drink?" I turned around to the counter and picked up a bottle of wine I'd been drinking and poured her a glass. We went into the garden and sat down.

"Smoke?" I said, and took out my cigarettes.

She shook her head and smiled. I lit one and turned to one side to blow the smoke away. She was still looking at me, keeping eye contact.

"Who you here with?" I said.

"Kim. She's my cousin."

I smiled and took another drag. She took a drink and left some red lipstick on the glass. We kept looking at one another.

"You're Andy Palmer, aren't you?" she said. "I've heard things about you."

I laughed. "None of it's true."

"Didn't you get caught drinking and doing drugs at church camp?" She raised her eyebrows.

I shrugged and took a sip of my wine.

"Kim warned me about you." She crossed her legs and smiled.

I took a drag of my cigarette and knocked the ash off the end.

She laughed. "But I think you're sweet."

She put her hand on my chest again and leant over to kiss me. I dropped my cigarette and held her hand and we kissed again.

"I'm cold," she said.

We grabbed another bottle of wine off the side and went to find a quiet spot to be alone, but all the rooms were full downstairs.

"Upstairs?" she said.

"Are you sure?"

She smiled, took my hand and led the way.

By the time we came back downstairs, I was hooked. The party was still going strong, so we sat on the stairs and shared the remains of the wine. I didn't want to let her go.

"You got a boyfriend?" I said.

"Kind of."

I took a gulp from the bottle.

"But things are weird," she said, and took the bottle and drank. "We won't be together much longer."

She passed me the wine.

"His dad's ill and he's dealing really badly with it."

I nodded. I didn't know what to say. Then I saw someone with their hands up to their face looking in through the glass in the door.

"Who's that?" Lena said.

They turned the handle and walked in.

"Andy?"

"Michael?"

"Where's Lee?"

"In the living room," Lena said, and we both pointed down the hallway.

"Looks like the party's over," I said. "Can I see you again?"

"Maybe."

I thought Lena was lovely and didn't consider how she had a one-night stand with me when she had a boyfriend. We never went on a date and only saw each other at parties. We talked on the phone and she introduced me to her mother when she hosted a party. So, in my mind, it was a blossoming romance and I was in love. But Lena never left her boyfriend.

Not long after, another Youth Camp came around and Lena decided to come. I'd taken a bottle of vodka to share with Jonny and, as soon as we got there, we had a few drinks in the room and went to check out the grounds of Sedbergh School and look for somewhere to smoke.

"How's things with Lena?" Jonny said, as we walked down the playing field beside a stone wall.

"Weird," I said, as we came to some trees.

"Not breaking up with you is she?"

I lit a cigarette and looked around at all the green space and beautiful stone buildings. "She's still with her boyfriend."

"She's messing you about."

I took a drag and blew the smoke up into the leaves of a tree. "This is a lot nicer than the schools near me."

"You should say something," he said.

I finished my cigarette and stood on it. Then covered it over with leaves. "I'm gonna talk to her tonight."

On an evening, there was a meeting similar to the ones we had on Friday nights except with louder music, a cooler band and smoke machines. Then we'd get the *don't do bad stuff; just love Jesus* preach from a forty-year-old in a surfer T-shirt, baggy jeans and bleached hair acting as if he's in tune with youth culture because he dresses like a ten-year-old and tells us *it's cool to go against the flow.*

Lena was outside the door talking to the girls from Church, so I went over.

"Can we talk?"

"The meeting's about to start."

"Can I sit with you?"

She came closer and lowered her voice. "Have you been drinking?"

I shrugged.

She looked away. "I need some space. You're always drinking."

I hung my head and kicked the gravel. "I need to talk to you."

"After, okay?" She smiled and squeezed my arm, then walked inside.

I watched her walk away and that moment at Lee's when we first met flashed before my eyes. I still loved her and thought it would all be fine. I walked back to Jonny and we went in and sat near the back.

As much as I didn't care about being involved in the meetings, I did enjoy the music and always got an overwhelming sense of warmth and joy in the atmosphere. And I felt it that night as the lights were dimmed and the band played. There was something there, but there was something stronger inside of me that said *not now, you can think about God later,* so I went back to thinking of Lena and scanned the room for her. She was sat with someone I didn't recognise. He was taller than me and looked a few years older. Everything about him was more mature – shirt tucked in, longer hair, shoes not trainers. She touched his arm, just like she had mine, and they looked at one another and smiled. I clenched my fists. *How could she do this?* I felt tears start to form. I hit the back of the chair in front of me. "I'm off for a fag," I said, and walked out.

I sat outside in the dark and smoked one cigarette after

another. I went over and over what I wanted to say to her and how I should act. *Should I shout and show my anger or be honest and show how hurt I am? What will she respond to?* I wanted to go back to the room and down the rest of the vodka, but I knew she wouldn't speak to me if I did. As the music died down and everyone started to talk, I went over and waited at the door for her. Nearly everyone I knew came out first and asked me if I was all right. Then when she did come, she was still with that guy.

"Lena," I said, and smiled when she turned to me.

She looked over at me, but didn't smile. She turned to the other guy and said, "I'll see you for a coffee." Then she came over to me.

I was so glad to be near her again that I almost forget to be angry and upset. We walked away from all the people and found a quiet spot behind the main building that looked over a garden. We stood near a wall that had trellises running up it filled with climbing roses.

"Who's the guy?" I said.

Her arms were crossed. "What do you wanna talk to me about?"

I walked closer to her and put my hand on her shoulder. "I thought we were together?"

"I've got a boyfriend, Andy." She shrugged my arm off her shoulder.

"You slept with me. I met your mum."

She unfolded her arms and looked over toward the garden. "I'm sorry."

I reached out and took her hands in mine. "I love you."

She didn't pull away.

"I like you too, but the drinking…" She looked down.

I put my arms around her waist, she put hers around my neck and looked up and gave me a slight smile. We hugged. Her perfume was there again: sweet, floral, beautiful. I kissed her and she kissed me back. I kissed her again, longer and softer, but after a few seconds she pulled away.

"I can't."

We stood apart, but still holding one hand. The hand that had touched my chest at the party.

I went to speak, but there was nothing to say.

"I've gotta go," she said.

Her hand slipped out of mine and she walked away.

I took a cigarette out and smoked it in deep drags before lighting another. *Bitch.* I grabbed at the trellis, yanked it from the wall, and threw it down. I jumped on it and kicked it, destroying the flowers.

Back in the dorm room, Jonny was talking to some of the other guys.

"Alright mate?" he said.

I walked over to my bed, picked up my case and opened it. The vodka was wrapped in a jumper at the bottom. I pulled it out, unscrewed the cap and drank. I counted five gulps before I stopped. My mouth filled with saliva and my jaw went loose. I fought the urge to throw up.

"What you doing?" He nodded his head towards the two younger lads.

"Who cares?" I tipped it back and took another long drink.

Jonny and the others were staring at me.

"Want any?" I held the bottle out towards him.

He shook his head. "What's happened?"

"I'll finish it, then." I screwed the lid on and walked towards the door.

Jonny grabbed his coat. "Wait, I'll come."

I shook my head and walked out, bottle in hand. I walked through the ground passing several people on my way to the wooded area at the bottom of the field. Everyone saw the bottle, but I didn't care. I sat on the floor and took a swig. I lit a cigarette and took a drag. I tried to steady my breathing. Hot tears ran down my cheeks. I took another swig, another drag. I cried. I drank. I tried to breathe.

I sat and I drank and smoked. I thought about Lena. I thought that hurting myself would make her feel bad and change her mind about me. So I kept drinking until the bottle was empty. *If she could see what I've done to myself, it might make her realise she loves me. I have to go and see her.*

I got up and walked toward the school. I knew she'd be in the dining hall having coffee with that guy, so I headed there. I walked past a group of girls from church and they shouted after me, "Michael's looking for you," but I kept going.

Someone must have grassed on me, but I didn't care, as long as I could get to Lena. I was nearly at the hall. Outside was full of people stood around chatting and drinking hot drinks. They saw me approach, wobbling, stumbling and covered in mud and leaves with the empty bottle still in my hand. They stopped talking and looked at me. I didn't care. I had to see Lena.

I steadied myself in the doorway of the dining hall. I wasn't ready for the bright lights and loud chatter. I looked and smelled different from everyone in there. The atmosphere was calm and filled with warmth and the smell of coffee and wood. But the panelling on the walls made it feel enclosed and I felt everyone's eyes on me as I walked in. I saw Lena at a table with that guy. They were sat with another couple and all four were laughing. I watched, as she looked at him and listened to him speak. Her smile. Her hand on his. She wasn't thinking of me. I stared, waiting for her to turn around and look at me. Then I felt a hand on my shoulder pulling me backward.

"What's going on?" Michael said. His brow was wrinkled and eyes wide.

"Leave me alone."

He looked down at the bottle and grabbed it from my hand. "Come on."

His arm was around my back and he was pushing me forward. I went with him, but not out of obedience. I knew

I couldn't be there. I couldn't watch her any longer. There was nothing I could do.

"What are you thinking?" he said.

I shrugged. I expected anger, but he was quiet and calm. We walked into the leaders' room and he sat me down.

"Coffee?"

I nodded. My eyes were still wet with tears, so I wiped them with my sleeve. My legs were shaking. He brought the coffee in and sat across from me.

"You know we'll have to send you home."

I nodded and took a sip.

"Do you want to talk?"

I shook my head.

"Can I pray for you?"

"I'm fine." I wanted to go that instant.

After the coffee, he took me to pack my things and wouldn't let me say goodbye to anyone. I knew then that I wasn't going back to Youth or camp or church. It wasn't working. It wasn't me anymore.

4

Walking through the village on an early, quiet morning was invigorating. It was summer, six a.m. and the sun was just coming up. The sound of birds chattering and my trainers crunching the gravel on the path were all that I could hear. As I neared the bakery, the smell of fresh bread became stronger until it enveloped me. I stretched on my hairnet, pulled my white baker's shirt over my head and went in.

"Don't just stand there, get some work done," said John, the owner, his gold medallion twinkling in the mess of black hairs at the neck of his shirt.

"What should I start on?"

"If you don't know by now, you might as well piss off home." He wiped the sweat off his brow with his forearm, then pushed his swollen stomach out and said, "Go and pack the pizza bases," and waved me away.

I'd been at the bakery two weeks and wasn't enjoying my first taste of working life. There were no scheduled breaks and if I went and ate a sandwich for more than ten minutes John sent someone looking for me. The only thing I had to look forward to was catching up with my mate Danny who was coming to the bakery on work experience.

But it wasn't much better when Danny did come, as he just talked and messed around.

"Should have seen Miss Fogarty trying to catch us on games. Proper stressed her out, she was running—"

"Get working. John'll be round."

"Chill out. Here, have a pizza." Danny threw a base, but I ducked and it hit the floor.

"Oi! Who's gonna pay for that, eh?" John walked towards us. "Stop screwing around or you can forget fag breaks."

I was glad when Friday came around, as it was Danny's last day. We were working away on the heat sealers as usual and singing along to the radio – "*Cruising down the freeway in the hot, hot sun. How bizarre, how bizarre*"– when we decided to go for a fag break.

We walked through the plastic strip curtains into the sun, brushed the flour from our clothes and went into the smoking shed. As soon as we'd lit up, Danny leant over the table and said, "Did you see that?"

"What?"

"On the side in the cooling area?"

I shrugged.

"That fat knob's wallet. Just sat there."

I shook my head and leant back. "I've gotta work here."

"Loads of people walk through there."

I stubbed my cigarette out. "It's not worth it," I said.

We walked back into the bakery and past the wallet. It was still sat there, untouched. We got back to our machines and carried on working. Every time we pulled down the handle on the machine it buzzed and we slid the packet off the side into a plastic tray. Down, buzz, slide. Down, buzz, slide. Little wisps of smoke floated up to our noses from the melted plastic, smelling like burning tires. Every now and again the heated wire would snap and need replacing. Danny pulled down the handle, it buzzed, but when he lifted it back up the wire was stuck to the pack and it was unsealed. He pushed the machine and said, "Screw this, I'm going for it."

Before I could say no, he'd gone. There was no one around and the place was quiet. Even the radio had been switched off. I stopped working and listened. I could hear the cars on the main road outside, but nothing else. I went back to sealing the packs of pizzas. But then I heard footsteps and stopped. They were confident strides. I was sure it was John. I looked around the corner, but couldn't see anyone, so I got back to work. Then I heard the swish of the plastic curtains and prayed it was Danny.

As he walked over to me, he pulled something out of his pocket and smiled. "Let's go," he said, and waved the wad of twenties in my face.

"I've gotta wait for John."

"Well I'm not getting caught," he said, and walked out.

I stood at the machine not knowing what to do. I thought John would think it was me either way, so I caught up with Danny and followed him out of the bakery and down into the park. We stopped at the bowling green and sat on the benches.

Danny slapped his palm with the money.

I took it and counted out a hundred pounds. "You thieving git."

"Beer?" Danny said.

So we went and bought some bottles of Thunderbird, Mad Dog, some cans of gas, pot, crisps and chocolate and sat in the park basking in the sun getting smashed.

But the following Monday I had to go back to work. I walked through the plastic curtains and John was stood there facing me with his arms folded. His eyes looked dark through his thick glasses. His hair was stuck onto his sweating forehead. He glared at me.

"Morning," I said, but my voice was almost lost among the sounds of mixers and ovens, "should I start on the bases?"

He kept staring at me. I couldn't look him in the eye, so moved down to see the gold sovereign hanging around his neck. He brushed the flour from the front of his shirt and said, "No, go home. I don't need you anymore," then turned and walked away.

Then I got a job at Fosters Bakery as a van lad. I was on the dock at five, on deliveries by six and home by eleven. Tony drove and I was the lackey, and we delivered bread to the villages around Holmfirth. Tony was in his mid-twenties and liked to call women *darling* and flash his toothy smile. We didn't get along.

I become friends with a van lad the drivers had nicknamed Jarvis, after Jarvis Cocker. He was a tall, pale and lugubrious ex-heroin addict who was flesh and blood evidence that *The Drugs Don't Work*. Heroin had left a huge gap in his life and given him insatiable habits – he couldn't smoke enough, drink enough or get laid enough. He was dripping in cheap Argos jewellery and had a ring on every finger, numerous chains around his neck and watches, bracelets and bangles jangling around his wrists.

We needed each other when out on the pull. Before meeting up with the drivers in town on Friday and Saturday nights, we'd get loaded on stubby beers that his dad brought back from France.

One Friday we were smoking outside the gates and he said, "Wanna go clubbing in Rotherham tonight?"

I took a drag. "What's up with town?"

"Nowt, but it's fifteen quid to drink all you want at Tivoli's."

"I'm in," I said, and stood on my cigarette butt.

We got a taxi to Rotherham with a bunch of Jarvis's mates. Tivoli's was an old stone building painted black and purple in an industrial area of the town with six bouncers on the door and even more inside. There were hundreds of people packed into the darkened space and only one door. It didn't look safe, but it was cheap. In the flash of the strobe light I could see the dusty surfaces and cracked plaster. It smelled like a cellar and was damp with stale beer. I stayed near the bar drinking anything from a bottle, so as to avoid the watered down rubbish in dirty glasses.

I felt a body next to me. "What's up, you grumpy sod?" the girl said.

I shrugged.

"Crap in here, innit?"

"Wish I'd not come." I laughed and took a drink.

She leaned over and kissed me. "What about now?"

"Getting better." I smiled and offered her a cigarette.

She took a drag and put her hand on my leg. "Wanna go outside?"

I nodded, downed the rest of my drink and followed her.

Later on, Jarvis came over and spoke into my ear, "That bird is one of the lads' exes."

I shrugged. "So?"

"He's gonna kill you."

In the taxi home I was stared at by a lad called Brett. I ignored him. But when we got out at Jarvis's, he walked over and said, "Think it's alright to mess with someone's bird?"

I took out a cigarette and lit it.

"Come on, Brett, leave it," Jarvis said, standing between us.

He came towards me, but Jarvis grabbed him.

"Come on," he said, gesturing me forward.

I backed away. "I'm getting off, Jarvis, see you Monday," I said, and set off walking down the street. It was only a fifteen-minute walk back home.

"Watch out," Jarvis said, and I turned to see Brett running towards me. I stiffened, expecting a punch, but his arms came up to my chest and he pushed me. I fell back, seeing the black sky above me, then hit my head on the curb and lost consciousness.

When I woke, the street was deserted. My head pounded, but

was soothed by the cold rain that was falling. Getting to my feet, I looked one way then the other, forgetting which end of the street of terraced houses was the way home. I touched the back of my head and an intense pain shot through me. I got angry at what had happened and hit out at a car wing mirror with my fist. The sound of the glass smashing echoed up the street, but nothing stirred. I carried on walking, then kicked the wing mirror off the next car. I felt better. I picked up pace and kicked another. Punched the next. Kicked. Punched. Kicked. Punched. Kicked. Punched. Until I reached the end of the street. I saw a couple of bedroom lights flick on and I started to run towards home.

As the rain got heavier, I looked for shelter. I tried all the car doors on the street I was on. I found one that was open and got inside. It was an old Peugeot that smelled of stale cigarette smoke. The footwell was full of food wrappers and every surface was thick with dust. I lay back and rested my eyes. The rain tapped on the roof and I lost myself in its rhythm.

I woke up, panicking, looking around to get my bearings. It was still night. Silent and still. The rain had stopped and all I could hear was my breathing. I lit a cigarette and leant back. Some of the plastic was flaking off the side of the seat next to me. I pulled at it. Then I burnt the pieces that were hanging off with my lighter. Watching them flare up and die out.

I'd always found burning things therapeutic. At my Grandad's I used to use his magnifying glass to melt crisp packets in the sun. With matches, I'd set fire to leaves and twigs in his back garden. Once, I took a box of matches to set bits of dry grass on fire in the fields at the bottom of my street. It had started with one patch of dry grass and one match. I'd wanted to see the flames consume it. I found it beautiful. I watched until that patch of grass was gone, but when I'd stamped it out more flames sprung up around me. I ran from one burning clump to the next, but they started quicker than I could stamp them out. Then the whole field was ablaze and the sound of horses whinnying in the paddock filled the air. I had to run. Then as the fire engines came to douse it, I joined the crowd at the end of the street and watched. I was terrified of getting caught, but fascinated by the chaos.

I lit a larger piece of the car seat and the smoke was blue and caught in the back of my throat, but I carried on. I held the lighter there for longer that time and the seat cover cracked and hissed. It burnt through into the yellow padding beneath. Then the flame took hold and its orange glow ate its way up the seat at speed. The pattern was consumed effortlessly, as the flame glided across it. I watched with satisfaction.

I reached over and tried to pat the flame out, but a blob of melted plastic stuck to my hand and I drew it back. It had fused to the back of my index finger and when I pulled it off the skin came with it. I watched as the flames got larger and more pointed. I had to get out of the car. There was no way I could put it out. I opened the door and fell onto the pavement. I watched for a minute, lying on the ground, as the car's innards were consumed. Orange flames were spreading into the back and out of the open door, licking at the paint. I knew it was only a matter of time before someone saw it, so I got up and walked away.

One of the drivers was getting married and he invited us all out for his stag do in Blackpool. We met in town at nine that Saturday morning. As soon as we were on the coach, Tony stood up in the aisle and said, "Who wants a beer, then?" and everyone cheered and the cans of Carling were passed around. Jarvis downed his in one, fashioned a pipe from it and we started on the pot.

Someone said, "Stick radio on," and we all sang along.

I get knocked down
But I get up again
You're never going to keep me down…

And the stag do started. We had burgers for breakfast when we got there, then headed for the pub. The first place was packed and we gave up on getting served after queuing for forty minutes. When we looked around we couldn't see the lads we came with. Jarvis said, "Let's find somewhere quieter," and we headed out.

We walked away from the seafront and into the town. The streets were littered with cigarette ends, empty burger wrappers, and stag and hen groups with matching T-shirts and hats. From behind us we heard someone shout, "Hey Jarvis, where you off?" and we looked around to see two of the drivers, Barry and Daz, behind us. We waited for them to catch up and told them we were off to find a quieter pub, so we didn't die of thirst. They decided they were coming too. We found a quieter place and sat down with our pints on some benches in the corner.

"Where's Barry?" said Jarvis.

"Talking to some Geordie bird at the bar," Daz said. "Can't tek him anywhere."

Barry came over with the woman and sat down next to me. "Shift up a bit, young 'un." They squeezed in next to me, so close that her leg was half on mine. I could see Barry's hand on her other leg, gaining ground toward her leather skirt.

"Where are yous from?" she said, as she ran a hand through her bleached blonde hair with inch-long roots.

"Barnsley," said Daz.

"Oh aye, bit rough there innit?"

Daz shrugged. We nodded and drank our pints. Barry started to whisper in her ear.

"Get off us," she said, laughing. Barry now had his hand fully up her skirt.

She gestured toward us.

"They don't care, love," he said, and kissed her neck.

Then they were all over each other and we tried to ignore them. I pushed her leg away from mine and she lifted it over Barry's knee. In doing so, her handbag dropped to the floor and spilled its contents, but she didn't notice. I reached down and started putting her purse and keys back in.

"Look at that," Jarvis said, and picked up a small medicine bottle that had rolled near his foot. He tried to read it, but it was too dark.

Daz was at the bar getting another round in, so I shoved her bag back on the seat and we headed to the gents.

Once in a cubicle, Jarvis peered at the label. "Jackpot!"

"What we got?"

Jarvis shook some green squidgy capsules out. "Benzos, man, jellies. Used to use these to come off the smack."

"Good?"

"Amazing."

"Here then." I held out my hand and he shared them between us. I had a small pile of green orbs sat in my palm. I was excited. "How many we doing?"

"Four, maybe six."

"Let's do six."

Jarvis laughed.

"It'll be fine," I said, and we downed them and pocketed the rest.

We went back into the bar and our pints were waiting for us on the table. Barry was still face-sucking with the Geordie and Daz started telling us stories from when he was a van lad.

A couple of women came near and said, "Howay man, we've gotta go."

"Alright, I'm coming," Barry's bird said, as she uncoupled herself from him and gathered her things. "See ya next time, lover," she said, and blew him a kiss.

We had another couple of pints and I noticed that I felt

calm. I was undisturbed water.

Jarvis turned to me in slow motion and said, "Alright, Andy?"

I opened my mouth to speak and the words took time to form, "Everything's slowed down."

His watery eyes glinted in the light from the table lamp. I turned around to look at the pub and saw a panorama of the bar room. The scene stretched from the bench where we sat, to the bar with people stood holding drinks, towards the glasses hanging at the end, then cigarette machines, toilet doors, the exit, and back to us. It curved around through a fisheye lens.

Barry stood up and downed his lager, "Come on, we've been ages."

"Let's chill for a bit longer," I said, but Jarvis got up and pulled me with him.

My legs were lead, but I pushed myself to leave. I couldn't tell how the drugs were affecting Jarvis from his face, as he always looked half stoned. As we walked along the street his legs were stilts and his arms cooked spaghetti. It was evening now and the coloured lights of clubs and food outlets lit our way.

We found Tony outside a bar. "Where've you been all aft?" he said.

"Hiding from you," said Barry.

We went into the club with Tony and joined the other guys.

"What you drinking?" Tony said.

"Laaager," I said.

He wrinkled his brow. "What are you on?" he said.

We drank and drank, passing from one place to the next and no-one questioned when me and Jarvis were falling into doorways and had to be kept upright when walking, as everyone was drunk.

Then I had a sense of greed, of wanting more of the

feeling that the tablets had given me earlier. So I took Jarvis to one side and said, "Let's down the rest."

He shook his head. "We'll be hammered."

"It's fine, come on." I got out the remaining capsules and swallowed them.

When I was a young, I was caught throwing balls of wet tissue onto the walls of the church toilets with my friend Jonny. He had suggested it, but I took it further by throwing them onto the outside wall until it was covered in white splodges. When the pastor's wife found out, she took me to one side and said, "Andrew, you always take things too far. If someone does one thing, you have to do it ten times!"

We went in and out of a couple more bars and I had to be escorted by the other guys. I was in the centre of the group being held upright and I kept drinking what people gave me. Faces floated before me, lights blurred and left traces in the air and music played on and on in an unrecognisable dirge of stretched notes.

Then I was alone.

I was stood against a metal pillar in a dark club with sweat stinging my eyes. I hung on, as I looked around with my head swinging from side to side. I couldn't see anyone I knew. I launched myself from the pillar to a table. Glasses and bottles dropped to the floor. I lumbered from the table to the wall and crawled along it to some stairs. There were three steps and then the doors leading outside. *I can do this. I can get outside.* I clung to the wall and placed a foot on the first step. Then stood and lifted my other foot. But the world spun. My head got mixed with my arms and legs and I didn't know which way was up. I lay at the bottom. I was crumpled paper.

"Get him out," one of the bouncers said, and they lifted me and threw me into the street.

I struggled up and fought my way through waves of people, grabbing hold of arms and shoulders. I fell, hit my head, walked into doorways, got pushed away. Then I found a quiet spot to lie down for a minute. Maybe five minutes, just until I sobered up a little. Just until everything stopped spinning.

I was on the street near the beach. It was daylight. My head rested on tarmac. Everything ached. My elbows were grazed, my jeans scuffed, and my pockets were empty. I rubbed my eyes to focus and felt a dull pain in my cheeks and nose. I pushed myself up. I was unsteady, but sober. I'd been lying in my own vomit, the same vomit that covered my shirt.

I walked from the deserted beachside to the town. It had to be early, as the town was dead. The first person I saw was a man opening shutters on a newsagent's window. He looked me up and down, then bent down to pick up a bundle of newspapers.

"Can I help?" he said, not looking up.

"Where can I catch the train?"

He lugged the papers up and leant them on the window sill. "North or South?"

I shrugged. "Barnsley."

"You'll need North. Straight along the front 'til you see the pier, turn right and follow the road. You'll see it." He smiled and nodded, then carried the papers inside.

I caught a glimpse of myself in the shop window. There was dried blood around my nose and mouth and my cheeks were bruised and grazed. I walked along the promenade in the direction he said. It bore the scars of the night before, but I knew I looked worse. At the station, I asked a member of staff if they could help me contact my parents and he took me to his office to use the phone.

After several rings, my dad answered.

"Do you know what time it is?" His voice was thick with sleep.

"I know, I'm sorry."

He mumbled under his voice and I could hear my mum in the background asking who it was.

"I need to get home and I've no money."

I heard a sigh and he told my mum I wanted a lift. "Okay, your mum says we'll come and pick you up. Where are you?"

"Blackpool."

Silence.

There was more mumbling and discussion in the background, then my mum came on the phone. "What's happened? Are you all right?"

"Can you just pay for a ticket or something?"

"You're sure you're all right?"

"I'm fine. I just need to get home."

After two years of working at Fosters, the bakery decided to streamline deliveries and the van lads were out. They offered us alternative work inside the bakery on twelve-hour nights, but me and Jarvis told them where they could stick that.

We completed our last ever delivery on a Friday and after a few pints with the drivers, I went over to Jarvis's. His dad had been to France on a booze cruise again, but he'd upped his game from crates of beer to big bottles of spirits.

"Look at this," Jarvis said, swinging a massive bottle of vodka around. "One and half litres." He passed it to me and I looked it over.

He brought in a couple of half-pint glasses and a carton of juice and we poured our drinks.

"To Fosters," I said, and took a drink.

"Good riddance," said Jarvis, and downed it in one, his bracelets rattling down his arm. He leant his head back, put his feet on the coffee table and shrugged. "Hated it there anyway."

I reached forward and refilled our glasses. "What now, though?"

"Now, we get hammered." He laughed and drained his glass again.

His dad came in and told us to be ready in an hour if we wanted a lift to town. Jarvis picked up the bottle and swirled it. "Think we could finish this by then?"

I shrugged, "Be rude not to."

Jarvis filled each glass half with the vodka and topped it with juice and we knocked it back. I poured us another, but even bigger, and we downed that.

He poured. We drank. I poured. We drank. It kept going until we had the remainder of the bottle in our glasses.

"Down in one?" I said.

Jarvis was taking a few deep breaths. "Maybe we should cool it."

His dad came through pulling his coat on.

"Come on, let's get it down," I said, and we finished it.

We got in the car and drove towards town. I was drunk, but not as drunk as I expected. But it was creeping up on me, bit by bit. His dad dropped us off outside a bar across from the bus station and we rolled out onto the pavement.

"Is he gonna be alright?" his dad said.

Jarvis was laughing. "Yeah, he's just pissed. Seen him like this loads of times." We wobbled into the pub with our arms around one another's shoulders. Jarvis went to the bar and I leant against the wall and lit a cigarette. My eyes started to swim and I felt like sitting down. As I smoked, I slid down the wall onto the floor. A middle-aged couple came over. "You okay, love? Want some water?"

I shook my head and smiled. "Fine," I said, but I had to force it out. I struggled to keep my eyes open and my cigarette rolled out of my hand. Jarvis came back with a beer, but the couple wouldn't let me take it. "He's had enough, you should get him home."

"He'll come round," Jarvis said, but then the barmaid came over.

"He's not staying here like that," she said, and tried to help me up. I put my foot underneath me and pushed with everything I had. Jarvis pulled one arm and the couple pulled the other. I was up. They walked me to the door and Jarvis told them I'd be fine and that he'd get me home. The couple left and Jarvis half dragged, half frogmarched me from the front of the pub to the back. I flopped against the wall and slid to the floor. I couldn't focus. A black curtain was slipping down in front of my eyes. I vomited on my clothes and shoes. I couldn't stand or sit, so I ended up lying on the ground. Jarvis pulled me up and dragged me towards the area at the back where the bins were and held me while I vomited again and again onto the street.

"What we gonna do?"

I couldn't answer. I tried to nod, but my head bobbed around.

"This is bad," he said, walking up and down in front of me with one hand on his forehead. I was lying down, watching his shoes pacing. I saw the tarmac stretching out before me, a sea of grey that seemed to be rocking.

"I'm gonna ring your parents, stay there."

He leant me up against the wall while he went to the payphone. I slipped sideways and my head landed onto a black bin bag full of rubbish. I felt numb. My feelings and sensations withdrew to a place deep inside. There was a weight in my body and mind that pushed me toward sleep. I wanted to let go and sink into it, drift off. But as I felt myself going, I pulled back and forced my eyes open.

What if I don't wake up?

I could see Jarvis in the phone box. He was motioning with his arms, pointing at me and pushing the hair back on his forehead. He caame back over and said, "They're coming. It'll be fine," but I heard the words from far off, as I sunk into the pavement and lost consciousness.

My parents drove through in a panic. They reached the spot where I was lying and dragged me into the car with help from Jarvis. They laid me in the footwell in the back. My mum was crying. My dad was white. She asked Jarvis what I'd had. He told her and she slammed the door and drove away. Jarvis stood behind the pub and stared as the car screeched down the street and around the corner.

At Barnsley Hospital, they pulled up outside A&E, flung the doors open, and dragged me into the corridor by my arms and laid me in front of the check-in desk. My mum went to the front of the queue and said, "I need help, my son, he's drunk, he's overdosed, help him."

My dad was in front of me pulling me up and sitting me against the wall, over and over again, but I kept sliding down onto the floor.

At the counter they said, "How do you know?

"I'm a nurse, just help him, please."

As they were asking my name and date of birth, my dad shouted and they looked over at me, lying on my back, vomit bubbling out of my mouth and over my cheeks.

"Turn him over," my mum said, as she ran over and pushed me onto my side and hit my back. Two nurses and a porter came through wheeling a bed and lifted me onto it. They took me through to a treatment room and went to get a doctor. My dad came with me and my mum went to move the car. Someone came and took my blood, but in the rush they left the tourniquet on and blood ran down my arm. My dad saw it and went to get someone.

I was alone.

I was lying on my back and I vomited again. It came up and out of my mouth, but I couldn't move. It ran back into my throat and blocked my airways.

I started to choke.

There was nothing I could do.

I couldn't breathe.

I couldn't move.

My dad came back and wiped the vomit from my mouth, sticking his fingers inside, but I still wasn't breathing. He tried to move me. He hit me on the back, but nothing worked. Then my mum came back. She reached for the suction machine on the wall and rammed the pipe down into my mouth, vacuuming the vomit from my throat and clearing the way for me to breathe. She hit my chest and waited. I took a breath. My chest moved. Up, then down. Up, then down.

And I breathed.

I breathed.

I breathed.

5

Twenty-four hours later, after having my stomach pumped, several drips administered, constant monitoring and the concerned faces of my parents looking on, I came around. I took the leaflets and advice from the doctor and agreed to an alcohol ban of at least three months.

We walked towards the car from the hospital, and I turned around to see the square building in several tones of grey. My mum said, "We love you," and took my arm.

"I love you, too," I said, and tried to smile.

She smiled for me and squeezed my arm. "It'll all be okay," she said.

I looked at her for a moment, then got in the back.

I watched out of the window as we passed through town. The college building on Old Mill Lane had the same block-of-flats style as the hospital. We passed under the railway bridge with its red and white peeling paint and orange rust. Then the rows of stone terraces gave way as the road widened and in the distance was the gasometer, a huge, rusty colosseum that dominated the landscape.

After a week of recovery, I knew I needed a job, so I bought the local papers. It was depressing. There was nothing I was qualified for except factory work. I carried on flicking until a small advert caught my eye.

Ever wanted to take time out and travel, but didn't know how? *The Year Off Handbook* **is the definitive guide to working and living abroad.**

I ordered the book, and within weeks I was boarding a plane to America. I'd bought new clothes, a backpack and stopped smoking.

That summer in Texas, the heat would get up to 41°C. I felt it the moment I stepped off the plane. A guy in a truck wearing a Stetson and mirrored glasses, picked me up. He threw my rucksack in the back and told me to sit up front. I watched the road as we headed down the highway. It looked dry and pale, and rippled in the haze. Cars were moving between lanes without indicating and everything seemed faster. Even the cadence of the road was unfamiliar.

When we pulled down the driveway, I could see the sprawl of it beneath me – sports fields, woods, lake, swimming pool, horses – Camp Hoblitzelle was huge. As soon as I was dropped off, I was ushered into a hall with lots of other teenage staff members for an orienteering talk by the camp leader.

He stood in the centre of the stage, walking up and down. "Hi, I'm Chip, Chip Hall," said the chirpy camp leader, "and I'd like to say a big welcome to ya'll at the beginning of this year's camp." He was tall, late forties and wearing a navy-blue polo shirt tucked into beige shorts, with a large overhang and sandals with long socks.

"Now, I'm sure we're going to have a super good time this summer, but I need to make you aware of a few camp rules, so we can all enjoy ourselves safely." His smile dropped and a wrinkle appeared in his brow.

"Number one, this is a Salvation Army camp and as such

we expect Christian behaviour at all times. No alcohol, drugs, cigarettes, cursing, or inappropriate physical contact, will be tolerated…"

He carried on talking, but I'd already stopped listening. Across the room from me was a girl. She was leaning on the wall with her arms folded. She had long pale legs and wore tiny denim shorts that were only just visible under her T-shirt. Her long hair was blonde and wispy. I had to meet her.

After the meeting, I set off walking to the back of the room to talk to her, but then Chip came back onto the microphone and said, "Could all new counselors meet me at the front, please?"

I headed to the small group and Chip held out his hand to me, "What's your name there liddle fella?"

"I'm Andy."

"Hi, *Ondy*." It didn't seem to compute that I was called Andy, but my accent made it sound different. "So whereabouts in England you from?"

"Yorkshire, in the North."

"Oh yeah, I heard o' there. York, it's a nice old city, right?"

"Yeah, but it's—"

"Sure, sure. Well it's good to meet you, Ondy. I've got you with Cavon in boys block 12. Cavon's just over by the door, so if you catch up with him he'll show you the way." Then he turned away to talk to someone else.

I walked towards Cavon and he said, "Wassup man, ah'm Cavon," and stuck out his hand.

We walked from the hall into the sun, and followed a track towards the boys' dorms. The heat made the air hum and I could hear the clicking of insects in the background. Cavon went through everything I needed to know, but all I was interested in was how I could meet the girl I'd seen. He told me that in the evening everyone went to the rec room to hang out if they weren't working, so that's where I planned to go.

I showered and changed my sweaty clothes, then headed out to the rec hall with Cavon. As soon as I walked through the door, I felt the air conditioning cool my body and wake me up. People were sat around the outside of the room talking, and a group were by the pool tables singing along to a song on the stereo. *"Wanna be a baller, shot caller, twenty inch blades on the Impala..."*

We walked over to the table and a guy told us they were getting ready to play a competition and asked if we wanted to join in. Two tables, two teams, the winner of each play one another.

"Usual rules, if you scratch on the eight ball you lose," the guy said.

"What's a scratch?" I said.

"If you're shooting a ball and the white goes in, that's a scratch."

I won my first couple of games and was feeling confident. Then I saw my next opponent. It was the blonde girl from earlier.

"This should be easy," I said.

She raised her eyebrows and put her hands on her hips. "We'll see about that." Her eyes were bright blue and her cheekbones had a light sprinkling of freckles.

"You wanna break?" I said.

"Go ahead. You'll need all the help you can get."

I broke off and potted a solid, but missed my next shot.

She pulled her hair back into a pony tail and lined up her shot. I could see the denim shorts under her T-shirt, as she leant over. She potted a stripe, then another and another, then missed. She looked over and smiled. "Not too bad, eh?"

I got down and potted all my solids and was on the eight ball. One ball to win. I lined up the shot and thought, *Should I let her win?* I adjusted slightly and the shot just missed.

She jumped up. "Ooh, so close."

The eight ball was in the middle of the table at the bottom, and the cue ball in the middle at the top. She took her shot slowly and the eight ball rolled into the bottom left pocket. She turned around to me and polished her nails on her shirt.

But the guys watching all went, "Ooohhh," and we turned to see the white drop into the bottom right pocket.

"Darn it," she said, and walked away.

"Wait," I said, and followed her, but as I got to the door someone called, "Hey, you won, you gotta play the next round."

A couple of days later, I bumped into Cheryl again. Cavon and I were taking our group of boys to their morning activity and Cheryl was the arts and crafts teacher. I spent all my time talking to her and letting Cavon deal with the kids. She was from Mississippi and I loved her Southern accent. I imagined her leant on bales of hay in a sunlit field with her denim shorts on and a checked shirt tied at the waist, tipping back her straw Stetson to let the sun warm her face.

From then on, we spent all our free time together and only fell out once when I went to a club in Dallas with a few of the guys. There was no drinking, as we were all under twenty-one, so all we did was play pool. But the next morning in the team building session, Cheryl wasn't talking to me and Chip was pacing the room.

Chip shook his head and said, "Oh my, oh my, oh my," then placed his hands on his hips, pushed out his stomach and scanned the room of faces avoiding eye contact with anyone in particular.

"I do *not* know what to say. Now I'm a reasonable man, but when I hear about camp rules getting broken by my staff, I just cannot believe it." He lifted up a hand and rubbed his forehead, closing his eyes. "Now, I'm not gonna name all the people involved in last night's situation, but suffice it to say, what these people did is not acceptable." He signed, put his arms behind his back and looked out of the window. He stood silently for a few seconds.

"Nightclubs are out of bounds. If I hear of anyone else going, they will be sent a'packing."

I went over to Cheryl, but she wouldn't look at me. I put my arm around her and she put her head on my chest. "I told you not to go."

We hugged, but as Chip walked by he made a motion with his hands for us to part, then walked past us shaking his head.

I went back to the dormitory and lay on the bed. The scratching and clicking of insects made me squirm and check my clothes. The lack of air con in the room left it smelling of insect repellent and stale sweat. I imagined lighting a cigarette and having a drink.

We were encouraged to socialise with the people we worked with, so Cavon invited me over to his house for the weekend. We had a barbeque, went shopping to a mall, and ate a Chinese meal so hot that I had to suck ice for a whole day. I tried to talk to Cavon and ask him what he planned to do with his life. He said he'd work hard at school, get good grades, stay out of trouble and become a Salvation Army officer. Everything he thought and did revolved around it. In the first month at camp we led a baseball match together, entered a chilli eating competition, got chased by an armadillo and stayed up late talking about girls. But then things went sour when I started hanging around with Rafael.

One afternoon, I was relaxing in the pool while the kids were having a swimming lesson. I had my arms outstretched on the side and my legs kicking the water in front of me. I could see the stables and almost smell the horses off to my right. In the distance, the lake was rippled and hazy in the sun's heat. The dry air was still, so still that the dust on the ground sat undisturbed and the blades of grass stood motionless. The heat was fierce.

"Nice tatt," Rafael said, and swum over and leant on the side next to me. He turned around, and between his shoulder blades was Rafael written in gothic script. "I'm Raf," he said, and put his arms behind his head. "Do you smoke?"

I lowered my voice. "Not here."

"Wanna come for a smoke in the woods later?" His eyebrows had vertical lines shaved into them, which made his eyes seem sinister. But the chance of getting a cigarette was worth the risk, so we arranged to meet later at the dorm. I wasn't sure why we needed to set a time and place to have a smoke, but he had the cigarettes, so I didn't argue.

Raf slipped into mine and Cavon's room without making a sound. "You ready, man?" he said, adjusting his beany hat.

We walked at speed behind all the dorms and around the back of a store of canoes, through which the sun left a dappled pattern on the ground. The path was dry cracked mud that made a crunching sound under our feet. The rattle of the grasshoppers grew louder the closer we got to the woods. I looked down and they were growing in number around our feet, so many that we were stepping on them as we walked.

"Do we need to go this far?" I said, looking back to see if the dormitories were visible.

"Just a bit further," said Raf, but we didn't stop until we were in the dense trees. He removed his hat and took out a pipe, a lighter and a plastic bag of weed. *Oh, a smoke.* He stuffed some into the pipe and lit it. After a few puffs, his eyes went milky and his lids drooped. He poked another clump in and passed it to me. I took a few draws on it and felt the comforting warmth wrap downy sheets around me. It was nothing like the resin we got back home, not nearly as harsh.

"One more? he said. We shared that pipe, and the chirping and humming of the forest floor became louder. The scratch and rattle of the grasshoppers rose and fell in a rhythm attuned to my movements. The heat fuzzed my body like static, as we laced back through the trees. I was Mr Soft, padding through a world wrapped in plump duvets. The smell of trees, water and smoke filled my nostrils and the dry earth crumbled beneath my feet, as we made our way back.

I went looking for Cheryl. I lumbered up to the window of the rec room and saw her reading in the corner. I knocked on the glass with both hands. She looked up and laughed, then gestured for me to come in.

"What's up?" she said.

I shrugged and smiled, but didn't speak. She was eating chocolate and drinking a can of root beer. I reached over and took them.

"Help yourself," she said, and laughed.

I gulped down the medicinal pop and munched through the chocolate. Cheryl stared at me. I grabbed her arm and pulled her up. "Let's play pool," I said, and flung her towards the pool table.

"What's wrong with you?" she said, but lowered her voice when people started to look. "That hurt."

I scooped all the balls into a mass in the centre and started whacking them in all directions. She pulled me close to her and looked at my eyes and smelled my clothes. She took me by the hand and led me out the back of the rec.

"Are you stupid? If you get caught…" She led me to the tennis courts. We were safe in there. It was getting dark and we were hidden by a fence. I lay down on the court with my hands outstretched, stroking the asphalt. I looked at the stars until all I could see was the black punctured with white pinpricks.

Cheryl was sat at the side on a chair. "How could you do this? she said, leaning back and putting her hair into a ponytail.

"Come and give me a kiss," I said, and tried to pull her onto the ground.

She moved away. "I'm serious. You'll mess everything up." She folded her arms and looked to the side.

I sat up and leant on the fence. "Let's not fight," I said, and reached for her hand. She held it, but still looked the other way.

After a few minutes, she came and sat next to me. We were still holding hands. She looked at me and smiled. "I don't want you to leave." She put her head on my shoulder and we looked at the sky and said nothing.

Every morning after breakfast, we had an outdoor chapel service in the wooden amphitheatre next to the lake. At the front where the speaker stood, was a large white cross that was visible from everywhere on camp.

That day, I sat further forward than normal and looked out at the blue water of the lake reaching into the distance toward the woods. The water was calm and flat, reflecting the sky with the shadow of the cross stretching through the centre. I listened as the speaker told us about the future and what God had planned for us. He spoke of the past being gone, but the future unset. That today was the only day we had to make a difference. That right now was the time to make a change. Then he said something that made me stop and listen. "God doesn't care about what you've done; he cares about what you're going to do." And I closed my eyes and put my head in my hands.

"God, I need help," I said.

I opened my eyes and looked through my fingers. Everyone was praying. No one was looking at me.

"I keep ruining everything and don't know what to do." I felt a tear slip off my top lip into my mouth.

"Please God, can you help me?"

I felt the heat of the sun grow and warm my back. I breathed.

"I'm worried about my future."

I looked at the floor and saw a shadow move across my feet, blocking the sun. A cold shiver ran through me. Then a hand touched my shoulder and I closed my eyes.

"Andy," Raf said, shaking me. I looked up and wiped my eyes. He gestured with his rail-track eyebrows towards the other side of the lake. "Woods in five?" Then he walked away towards the exit.

I sat for another minute, but the moment was gone and the meeting was ending. I got up and walked from the amphitheatre towards the woods. I felt my stomach tighten.

Raf had invited another guy along called Chad, who was wearing a T-shirt several sizes too big for him and basketball trainers. He put his hand in the air for me to grab and said, "Dude, we're gonna get stoned."

"Shut it, Chad," said Raf, under his breath, and punched him on the arm.

We walked until we got to the same part as before. We shared several pipes and I watched as Chad fought to keep his eyes open, but they drooped so low that he looked half asleep.

"Dudes, I'm wasted," he said, and leant over with his hands on his knees.

I looked on the floor for the biggest grasshopper I could find, then put it on his neck.

In slow motion, he opened his eyes and turned his head. "What the hell?" He stood up straight and shook his T-shirt, "Get it off." He spun around and screeched.

Me and Raf fell about laughing.

"Damn guys, that was intense," Chad said. "Eat these." And he picked up a handful of grasshoppers and threw them at us.

We jumped away, but they clung to us, so we pulled off our shirts and batted the insects away.

"Chill man, chill," Raf said, and we stopped to catch our breath.

When we got back to camp, Chad and Rafael went off in opposite directions and I went to the dorm to lie down.

During breakfast the next morning, I was summoned to Chip's office.

As I walked in his secretary said, "Take a seat honey, he'll be right with you." I could hear him behind the door, laughing and talking on the phone. My hands were shaky and wet with sweat. A red light flashed on the desk and the secretary told me to go in. I knocked, and opened the door. The room was wood panelled and in the centre sat Chip behind a huge desk. He gestured with his hand saying, "Come in Ondy. Take a seat." His smile was wide and showed the contrast between his bright white teeth and tanned face. "How you doing?"

I smiled, but knew we weren't here for a catch up.

"Good, good. Well thanks for coming by Ondy, I appreciate it." He leant back on his chair and made a dome with his hands. "Do you know why you're here?"

I glanced at the wall behind him. There was a framed picture of him and his family dressed in Native American clothes with painted faces, feathered headdresses, and suede tassels. They had their right palms facing out and at the bottom it said, '*How, from the Halls.*'

"Look Ondy, I'm not gonna go over every rule you've broken, but I'm going to say this. I think you're a nice guy who's clearly great with kids. People like you, but you're maybe used to," he moved his hands in the air, searching for the words, "more freedom." He looked at me, scanning my face.

My stomach was a rock. I knew what was coming. I'd been in this situation many times before. There was nothing I could say or do. I knew his mind was made up.

"Maybe you have habits or desires that you want to pursue, but we can't allow here. Understand?" His smile was wide and he held out his arms and raised an eyebrow.

I thought of Cheryl. I thought I'd never see her again.

"Look, bottom line, we feel your presence is a bad influence on the younger people, so we've made arrangements. Your flight is in two days."

He stood up and waited for me to stand. I felt numb, but struggled to my feet. He came around the desk and faced me, his smile still wide. He shook my hand then passed me a cardboard box. I felt his hand at my back, ushering me toward the door and out of his room.

"And on behalf of everyone at Camp Hoblitzelle, I'd like to say a big thank you for all you've done for us," he said, and shut the door.

I walked from the office in a bubble. My feet hitting the ground shook my body, but I heard nothing. I started to cry. Inside the box were several T-shirts that all said Camp Hoblitzelle on in different designs. I picked them out one by one, and dropped them onto the grass on the way towards the dorm.

Cheryl saw me and came running over.

"What happened?" She looked at the trail of T-shirts behind me, from them to me, and back again. I didn't have to tell her.

She looked down and kicked the grass. "What about me?"

"I'll put you in my rucksack, no problem," I said, and laughed.

"I wish you could." She smiled then took my hand. We hugged. She walked me back to my dorm, then went to teach a class.

At the dorm, I shook off my upset and started thinking of home. I called my parents and told them I'd messed up. There was no anger in their voices, just disappointment. That made it worse. I could have stayed in America for another month on my visa, which I'd planned to use to travel, but instead I was going back home early.

Later, Raf told me that Chad had got the munchies after we got high, broken into the kitchen, and stolen a five-litre tub of ice-cream. The cooking staff found him sat in the middle of the floor eating chocolate chip with his hands. We'd never have got caught otherwise.

The next two days passed in a blur, and I spent every minute I could with Cheryl. On the night before I left, we had one last game of pool in the rec. Cheryl won, but she didn't celebrate. I took her hands and pulled her close to me. I kissed her and tasted a tear on her lips.

"I'm really gonna miss you," she said, and put her head on my chest.

I hugged her.

We walked outside onto the veranda and sat against the wall overlooking the camp. Street lamps lined the sides of the roads and tracks, that weaved through the camp. All the buildings were lit up, but the surrounding countryside was black. I wasn't cold, but I felt a shiver down my spine. The stars filled the sky, and I looked up and tried to lose myself in them like when we sat in the tennis court. But I felt grounded by the weight in my stomach. My head swam with thoughts of home and how when I was back I could drink these feelings away.

"Will you come and visit me?" she said, her head still on my chest.

"I want to," I said, but I wanted to let her go. It was too much.

"I'll be heartbroken when you leave."

I went to speak, but couldn't.

"I'll always remember this as the best summer I've ever had." She turned her face into my shoulder.

"I'm sorry," I said, and I was. Sorry for hurting her, sorry I'd never see her again, and sorry that I'd dragged her into my mess.

"I wish we had more time together," she said, and closed her eyes and snuggled into me.

I held her, and looked out over the grounds. The night was still and quiet, except for the clicks and rattles of the insects. The air was soft and warm. In the far distance, I could see the lake. A black, flat mass surrounded by buildings and the forest dark and forbidding behind it. In front, stood the amphitheatre with the large white cross at its centre. The cross was lit at its base and it glowed iridescent against the deep black of the lake's water.

6

I watched the wet monotony of the road through a rain-streaked window on the journey home from Manchester. The M62 was nothing like the highway in Texas. From the dark grey of the tarmac to the mid grey of the sky, the colourless landscape felt heavy and dull. I looked down at the duty-free bag between my legs and wished I could open a bottle of whisky right there and then. As we hit a bump in the road, the bottles clinked.

"Back on the booze, then?" my dad said, as he turned around and looked at me. His face was clean-shaven and his hair parted on one side. He wore his uniform of button-down oxford shirt and crew-neck jumper.

Before I could answer, my mum said, "Just leave it," and placed her hand on his thigh. He turned back around.

The day before felt like a lifetime ago. Sitting with Cheryl looking out over the camp, was now just a picture in my mind. I couldn't remember the feel of the heat or the sound of the grasshoppers.

My dad turned around again. "You need a job. We're not having you sitting around drinking all day."

I reached down to the bag and touched the top of a bottle.

Something stopped me taking it out and drinking from it, but just holding it made me feel calmer. "I'm going to college," I said.

My mum looked in the rear-view mirror and smiled. My dad grunted.

College wasn't enrolling for another month, so I spent my days playing snooker and drinking. I got a job behind the bar at The Green Man in the evenings, where I drank the booze when no one was looking.

When September came around, I enrolled at Barnsley College and on my first day I bumped into an old friend I hadn't seen since primary school.

"I know you, dun't I fella?" he said, pushing his long hair from his eyes.

"How's things, Jim," I said. "Fancy a pint?"

We went over to The Union. A dark and dingy bar across from college where the beer was cheap. We got our drinks and looked for somewhere to sit. Jim saw a girl he knew and started walking towards her.

"Alright Ange, how's tricks?" he said.

She was sat arguing with a guy, but stopped as we sat down.

"Tell Gav to stop bugging me about speed, I've told him I've none left," she said, grinding her teeth and barely parting her lips.

Jim shrugged and looked at me and shook his head.

"Come on Ange, you've always got summat," Gav said.

"Doctor's put me on all these tablets and I've no idea why," she said, her eyes wide and pupils dilated. "I don't need any of 'em. I'm happy with my beer and speed." She pulled her handbag up onto the table and started pulling out box after box of pills.

Gav started picking up the boxes and reading them one by one, then throwing them back down.

"What they got you on?" Jim said.

"Chuff knows. Some for depression, some for anxiety, some for sleeping, some for my back… It's stupid really, a bit of speed perks me up every time, but they won't prescribe that, will they? I mean, look at all these. Loads of the flipping things. I'd be rattling like a moneybox if I took 'em all…" she said, and kept going whether we were listening or not.

"Bet those wouldn't make you babble like speed, though," Jim said.

We laughed.

Then Gav looked to have found something. "How much for the zimmers? Tenner a box?" he said.

She thought for a minute. Then shrugged. "Alright. Buys me drinks all day."

Gav offered us some and Jim bought a strip. He popped some out and pushed four pills towards me. "Only sleeping pills," he said. So I threw them into my mouth and gulped them down. Then Jim took four and Gav swallowed the rest of the box.

"Steady on, Gav," Jim said, but Gav shrugged and lit a cigarette. He passed them around and we all lit up, and Ange kept talking.

I felt drunk, but I'd only had a pint. I could feel myself swaying where I sat, so I put my hands out and steadied myself on the table. My eyelids were getting heavy. I looked at Jim and he looked fine, but Gav was leant sideways with a string of drool hanging from his top lip. We decided to go for a game of pool and I nudged Gav to see if he wanted to come, but all he could muster was, "Two minutes." We went upstairs, dragging our bodies along the wall of the narrow steps pulling off flaked paint and bits of plaster. When we got to the pool machine, we couldn't get the twenty pence pieces into the slots and kept falling backwards onto the floor when we tried.

"Feel like I've drunk ten pints," I said.

Jim put his arm around my shoulders. "Good aren't they,

fella?"

He got down to break off, but the cue just missed the white and slid out of his hands onto the table. It was my turn, so I flipped it around and hit the ball with the fat end of the cue. The yellows and reds split and bounced around the green cloth making a pattern my eyes couldn't adjust to.

"Right, I'm gonna get one in," said Jim, and he aimed a shot up, pulled the cue back and fell sideways onto the ground. We called it a draw and headed back down the stairs for another pint, scraping ourselves down the wall again. We joined Ange at the table, but Gav was gone. The pills had made the beer taste metallic, but we still managed another couple of pints. After that, I got drowsy and started to slur my words. I kept closing my eyes and drifting off, only to wake up with a start ten seconds later with an image of my bed fading away.

"I'm gonna lie down," I said, and slipped onto the floor under the table.

Jim tried to pull me up, but Ange said, "Let him sleep it off for a bit."

So I lay there with my face on the cool ground, and rested. But then there was a commotion and the doors of the bar opened, sending triangles of light spreading across the floor towards me. Several pairs of heavy boots tramped through the room towards the back, then returned thumping past me a few minutes later. I was singing a song I'd made up. "Slimy, slithery snakes, sliding on the floor, slimy shiny slithery snakes slipping through the door." But Jim kicked me. "Ssshhh," he said, "do *you* wanna get arrested as well?"

Then I caught a glimpse of Gav being led out into the daylight by two policemen. His hands were cuffed behind his back.

"What a pillock," Jim said.

Ange sat up straight and raised her eyebrows. "Who?"

"Gav, you dozy mare," said Jim, "but who sold him the pills?"

"I didn't expect him to nick a microphone stand, did I?" Ange said, grinding her teeth.

The next day, he took me to scour the grass of Locke Park for magic mushrooms, eating them fresh from the ground. "Only out in September, so we might as well have at 'em," Jim said. So we did.

One morning, he was sat in the garden strumming his guitar to *Nowhere Man* while it played on the stereo. He invited me in for a cuppa. We took our tea upstairs to where the bong was set up and Jim started to prepare it. As he pulled the bottle up, the vacuum from the water drew thick yellow-white smoke plumes into the chamber.

"Here fella, this one's yours."

The hit was instant. I felt sick, and warm all over. I tried to stand, but I weighed twenty stone and was stuck to the floor. So I lay back and closed my eyes. I started to spin, my whole body revolving. It got worse when I closed my eyes, so I opened them to see Jim blowing the smoke out from his bong and holding the bottle for me.

"Come on, I've got another thick yellowy one for ya."

I got down and filled my lungs, then crawled onto the bed and curled into the foetal position to slow down the spinning. *Being for the Benefit of Mr. Kite!* flicked round on the CD player and when it got to, *"and of course Henry the horse dances the waltz…"* the music rolled and whirled, so we did forward rolls on the bed around and around in circles until we fell about laughing, breathless.

Jim picked up his guitar and blasted *Voodoo Child* in my face, pressing me into the couch. I closed my eyes and started to see colours coming from the depth. I was staring into space. Into pure blackness. Twists of light snaked through the void dancing in slow motion. Stars came racing at me followed by swirls of colour vibrating with the twang of the guitar strings. They moved, following the music, speeding and slowing, changing shape and pattern, turning into molten liquid bubbling and overflowing, at once bright and shining then thick, bulbous and dark. He switched songs and I was speeding a car down an infinite road with the heat of the sun on my face and a breeze in my hair, and in the distance the lapping of a wave tickling my ears.

The music stopped, and I opened my eyes. "Got me proper tripping then, man."

Jim laughed and put his guitar down. "Music's like that." He went over to a chest of drawers and pulled out a plastic bag filled with sheets of colourful paper. "But that's not a real trip."

On the paper I could see the Warhol headshot of Marilyn Monroe with pink skin and yellow hair on a blue background. I stared at them. "How strong is it?"

"Chuff knows. Been taking them every day for a week and haven't had a bad one."

I looked at them again. I'd fantasised about taking it and now it was right in front of me. "Will it change me?" I said.

He laughed. "Will it chuff."

"Gimme two, then."

"Try one, you don't wanna get like Lennon, he was eating 'em on his cornflakes."

I put the square of paper onto my tongue like it was communion bread, and waited for the ceremony to begin.

"How you feeling? Jim said.

There were waves of tingling spreading through my body and clarity in my mind. "I feel like we've gone back to the sixties," I said.

Jim laughed. "Last week I took a few and saw Marilyn Monroe dancing towards me with her arm out." He picked up his guitar and sang.

She bangs a drum and makes it heaven for me
I give a smile there's still a possibility
She held out her hand as if to ask me to dance and

79

Suddenly it's 1960 and I feel American.

Whoa ooa Marilyn…

And it all made perfect sense to me. We were meant to feel American and like we were in the 60s. That's why we had acid with that image on it. It was meant to be. Everything felt neat and tidy and in its place. I was sat in a chair that held me just right, and Jim was cross-legged on the floor playing his guitar.

I lit a cigarette. The smoke filled my lungs then flowed out. It was calming and satisfying. "I love how the smoke twists and curls from the end and lights up like a beacon when you take a drag," I said.

Jim laughed. "Liking it then?" he said.

It was so gentle. It just crept up on me. I stared at the gap in the curtains and the shaft of light in its centre. The dust particles were dancing in the glow and I thought, *everything is moving, everything dances.* I opened the window to feel the air. It was crisp and fresh. I breathed to see my movement and to watch as my breath plumed from my mouth and travelled upwards to join the clouds. *Nothing wasted, everything connected.*

Jim got up and leant his guitar against the wall. "Wanna cuppa?"

We walked downstairs to the kitchen and I took a seat at the dining table. I lit a cigarette. As the kettle was boiling, Jim was chatting and walking around the small kitchen in front of the table making repeated patterns in the air with his body. I watched, fascinated, as the colours and textures of his clothing left a mark in the air where they'd been, then faded slowly.

I looked down at the cigarette hanging between my fingers and was shocked to see that it had burnt all the way down to the filter. *But I only lit that a second ago*, I thought. Jim caught me staring at the remnants of the cigarette that I'd not taken a drag of, and laughed. I looked at him and started laughing too. "I need the toilet, mate," I said.

While washing my hands, I looked up into the mirror. It was me, but in stuttered snapshot images. Every time I moved, another photograph skittered into the frame in front of me. I laughed, and got an open mouth shot; I frowned, and got a brooding brow-wrinkled look; I picked up a dog's lead and hung it around my neck and made a confused face.

The sliding door of the toilet opened. "What you doing, fella?" Jim stood there, door handle in his right hand, letting reality into my dream. "Come on, let's eat."

He made ham and mayonnaise sandwiches, followed by green apples and cups of tea. They all tasted extraordinary. I enthused about the freshness of the apple, that it was a drink and food all rolled into one and that the colour was pure neon.

"Let me show you some tricks," Jim said, and he placed his arm down on the table with his palm facing up. "Look at my veins. See the blood pumping through them, moving up and down like mini blood motorways?"

I looked, and saw movement under the skin. The blue, raised channels were moving blood up and down in rhythm to my heartbeat. Then Jim said, "They've stopped," and they did. Then I looked at the wooden top of the table and I could see the lines in the grain pulsing under its surface towards the knots. The life and energy in his arm was in the table. Life was in all things. Everything had the same electricity and spark.

"Dunno why people think drugs are bad," I said. "They feel good and let us see stuff."

"Control, fella. They want us all thinking the same and living the same," said Jim.

"Spose we need some rules, though."

"Rules, conditioning. It's their way or nowt."

We moved to the living room and lay on the carpet. It was already dark outside. The day had flown by.

"Booze and fags are drugs," Jim said, "but society says

they're fine. There's no logic to it. Drugs were here before laws."

I stared at the ceiling. The rings of Artex swirled of their own accord. "Everything's limitless. We're like tiny specks, but part of it all."

"People need acid," said Jim.

I waved my hand in front of my face and watched the trails left in the air. "I wish we could see angels like Blake did," I said.

Jim laughed and sat up. "What we on about? I'll put *Fantasia* on, it's amazing when you're tripping."

We watched Mickey Mouse prancing across the walls in a gown, waving a wand. The TV couldn't contain the pictures and they went where they liked. The sound was flowing out into us like a river with different temperatures and textures that we could feel. We were part of the cartoon and the living room was another world.

Later, Jim went up to bed. Things had become flatter and less vibrant. All colour was sapped from the room. The full strength of night had settled in and it was cold. I needed rest. I climbed onto the couch and tried to sleep. It wouldn't come. I could hear every minute noise, so I used cushions to block out all sound from my ears. But then I could see light, so I used the furniture seats to block that too. Then I lay there and tried to think of nothing.

At The Green Man, we had a rule that all tips were to go into a jar and be shared between bar and kitchen staff at the end of the night. But I always pocketed mine. At Christmas, an empty coffee jar was taped shut and a slit cut in the top. All tips throughout December were to be put in and the lot shared out at the end of the month.

It was a week before Christmas, and I had no money to drink and no time to do it. I was down for every shift – Christmas eve, Christmas day, boxing day – and I didn't get paid until the end of the month. And I wanted to drink. I needed to drink. I saw that the tip jar was getting full. I lifted it up and looked through the slit to see lots of folded notes. I shook it, but nothing came out. The slit in the top was flexible, so I squeezed my middle and index fingers in and pincered a note out. I did it again and again, until I had three hundred pounds. My heart raced.

I called Jim when I got home, told him about the money and suggested a piss up. There was just the issue of getting out of work. I called my boss, Greg.

"What's up, I'm in the middle of prep?" I could hear the thud of hard vegetables being chopped.

"I'm not coming tonight." My heart was racing.

"Yeah, yeah, good one Andy. Nice one."

Say it, then you're free.

"I'm not coming back. I'm done."

"What the… Why?" I heard his knife hit the metal table. I had no answer.

The line went quiet. I could hear his breathing. Deep, determined breaths that he snorted down his nose.

"At Christmas?"

I couldn't speak.

He slammed the phone against the table, over and over again, then said, "You selfish little—" but I put the phone down. I didn't want to hear it. I felt bad, but booze came first.

We took a taxi to a posh hotel.

"What we drinking?" Jim said.

"VCRs?" I said, and headed to the bar.

"What're they?"

"Cocktails. Meant to blow your head off."

We sat in a corner in leather chairs and smoked. We ordered the vodka, champagne and Red Bull, and relaxed. Then we bought brandy in large snifters and swilled it around and sipped it, while smoking cigars.

"You won the lottery or summat? A guy turned to us.

"No mate," I said, "we're in a band."

Jim put his head in his hands.

"What kind of music?" he said, and pulled up a chair next to us.

Jim looked over at me and rolled his eyes. I poured the guy a glass of champagne.

"Doors tribute band. Riders on the Storm," I said.

The guy came closer to me and said, "My brother's got a recording studio."

Jim got up and went to the toilet.

"I could get you some studio time at a discount if you like." He picked up one of our cigars off the table and looked at me.

I smiled and he lit it.

Jim came out of the toilet and went to the bar. He bought some bottles of wine and brought them over. I took a bottle of red and started drinking it from the bottle. A few more people came and joined our table, wanting to hear about our rock band. I felt out of my depth, so put on a show by downing my bottle of wine and starting another.

"Let's go," Jim said.

"Got a rehearsal tomorrow," I told everyone, as he dragged me out.

When the taxi came, the driver refused to take me, as I was standing up in the back singing, *"Break on through to the other side, break on through to the other side, yeah."* But Jim convinced him, and we slumped in the back drinking the leftover wine.

My parents booked a holiday, and I stayed at home with the place to myself. I bought booze with the money they gave me for food, and aimed to be wasted the whole week.

On the morning of the first day, I started drinking beer with my breakfast, and once I was drunk, I went out for a walk. I wandered around the village with a half bottle of Jack

Daniel's in my back pocket, topping myself up as I went along. I'd planned a drug binge with Jim that evening and he was picking me up at six with his cousin and some pot, speed and acid. But I couldn't wait till then. I wanted to be high right away, so I went to see Brent. He was in one of his usual spots in the beer garden behind The Red Lion.

"Brent," I said, waving him over, "how's things?"

"Andy." He nodded, and put his pint down on the wall.

I checked no one was near. "Got any speed?"

He took a drink of his pint and put it down on the wall. "All I've got are these." He pulled out a bag filled with pink pills from his chest pocket and shook them. "Pink hexagons. Three for a fiver."

Back at home, I poured a long drink of vodka and lime, placed an E on my tongue, and gulped it down. I was sure it would wear off by the time Jim came by later. I put my feet up, flicked on the TV and waited.

Nothing happened.

I drank a few beers, but still felt nothing except the alcohol. I thought, *screw it* and took another pill.

Not long after, waves of warmth lapped up my legs. I was sat on a beach, legs outstretched into the water. My stomach turned into a jellyfish and floated off. The rest of my body shifted in the current. I gulped down bottles of cold Mexican beer while the heat of the Mexican sun burned inside my belly, rising to my skin's surface and setting me alight. Invisible strings jerked my body to a rising and falling sound like zeee oooo zeee oooo zeee oooo. I was enjoying it so far.

Was it the second pill that did it, or has the first just kicked in? If it's the first that's just kicked in, the second is coming and I don't think I can take it.

I panicked and went to the kitchen to drink lots of water. Then it turned menacing.

Walking back through to the living room, I was fighting my way through a tight vein. Wading through platelet-thick blood moving in the opposite direction, and through a valve that was unyielding. I pushed through and was released onto the couch that sucked me in like the last flick of spaghetti into the O of pursed lips.

As a boy of eleven, holidaying in Devon with my parents, I slipped off a ledge at high tide and into deep water. Not expecting such depth, my casual plunge sunk me several feet over my head and the spasm of my lungs sucked in the salty water. Instant panic hit my gut, but my body wouldn't respond. I lolled in the undercurrent with the light of day fading above me. Pressure under my armpits raised me up and out. A woman pulled me back onto the ledge, scraping the skin of my stomach on the rock.

I didn't even see the ledge this time. I'd jumped off with that same casual attitude and found myself unable to swim to safety. I was in so deep, so quickly. Fear grabbed me with two fists curled into the front of my shirt. It was the same fear you have when you've swum too far out and don't think you can make it back to shore. And no one is there to signal for help. It's the fear that causes involuntary urination and the demobilisation of all your limbs. What scared me the most, was my inability to move my mouth. I tried to speak and vocalise my fear and frustration in the hope I wasn't too far out to get back to safety. But my mouth wouldn't move and I couldn't talk.

I couldn't talk.

I could not talk.

I have a phobia of walking on piers with gaps in the boards showing the water beneath. I rarely go on boats. I love the coast, especially beaches, but it's the impenetrable dark of deep water and its mysterious currents that strike fear into me.

When I was six, my uncle went missing off the coast of the Isle of Man while out sailing. He was gone for six weeks, before his body washed up on a Scottish beach. His boat had sunk, after hitting floating debris.

Now I was sinking. Water filled my lungs and no sound would come from my mouth. Nothing would hold still. Not the floor, not my line of sight, not the TV or the fireplace, not thoughts or images. I was a new-born calf flailing around. I stumbled to the floor. I felt myself welling up, but tears couldn't crack my porcelain face. I was scared for my life and my only hope was seeing Jim and his cousin soon.

I heard a knock like it was far off or in a dream. I dragged myself off the couch and forced my numb body towards the door and opened it. Jim's face and that of his cousin were huge and carnivalistic, with wide smiles and round heads. I stared. I still couldn't speak. I tried, but my lips slowly bumped into one another while my face made no expression. *What if I've had a stroke?*

"What's up, fella?" Jim said, staring into my face.

Help me! I said with my eyes.

He turned to his cousin and said, "He's messed up. Looks like Lurch."

He turned back to me and said, "What you had?"

I tried to speak, but still nothing came.

Jim's cousin said, "Seen people like this on ket. Bet he's a million miles away."

I took the third pink pill out of my pocket and held it out. Jim took it and looked closely. "Look at the brown flecks of smack. You're gouching, big time."

"Let's get off," his cousin said. "I don't wanna be here with him like that. Not with all this." He patted his pocket.

"Don't stress. We're going now," Jim said.

Jim turned to me. "We're off down to mine for summat to eat. We'll come back in a bit."

I was screaming at him, *don't go, I need your help, just wait here till I feel better, please!* But it was all inside my head, he couldn't hear any of it.

They started walking down the street, but Jim turned around and saw me standing in the doorway. "It'll wear off in a bit. Get inside."

Please stay, please stay, please stay, I said, but my anaesthetised mouth didn't move. I turned and went back into the house. I was alone.

I was trapped.

I waited and waited, but instead of getting sober, I got worse. My whole body was becoming useless. I couldn't stay in the house any longer. I knew I had to get help, but I couldn't call an ambulance. I was terrified of what could happen. Jim had seen heroin in the pills and his cousin mentioned ketamine. They could be fatal and time was running out, so I decided to go and find help.

I got out of the front door by clinging to the wall and then the drainpipe. I stepped down onto the driveway and noticed I had no shoes. There was no way I could put shoes on, so I kept going holding onto cars, hedges and walls. Sweat stuck my shirt to me, but I felt cold.

I was heading to Jim's. I didn't know where else to go in that state. Even fearing I may die, I didn't want the neighbours involved. It took a long time to get to the bottom of the street. There was no way I could get to Jim's house two streets away. My vision was cloudy and I wanted to sleep. I couldn't carry on. I found a wall and leant against it. But my legs weakened and lost sensation. I slipped to the floor. I knew my face was in gravel, but there was no pain.

Someone will find me, I thought, and let myself go.

I heard voices coming towards me.

"Who's that on the floor?"

"Dunno."

"Let's check."

"He looks terrible."

"Is it..."

"It's Andy."

Then they surrounded me. "What's wrong? Can you hear me?"

I couldn't speak, get up, move my arm, nothing. But I made a groan as loud as I could, and hoped it was enough.

"He's soaked with sweat. Let's get him home."

I felt tugging and pulling in my arms. They were carrying me. I was chainmail – heavy, cumbersome and limp. They dragged me back to the house and flopped me onto the bench in the back garden. People were milling around, panicking.

"Should we call an ambulance?"

"Let's call Michael."

I felt safer then. People were helping me. I thought I'd be all right. The bench was hard and I couldn't move, but help was coming.

Lights, the sound of an engine approaching at speed, a car door slamming.

"Andy, can you hear me? It's Michael. I'm gonna help." He was knelt beside me with his hand on my head. "Can you open your eyes? Can you tell me what's wrong?" He pulled back my eyelids and I tried to hold them open. I groaned again. "I'm calling an ambulance." He stood up, but he was still close.

"Ambulance, please."

"No, a young man."

"Andy."

"He's unconscious."

"He stinks of booze, but I don't know."

"I'll try and ask."

He knelt down again and pulled me up into a seated position. "How much have you drunk?"

I couldn't answer.

"He can't answer, just get an ambulance here."

"Water. Okay."

I felt his hands in my pockets. My keys. A few minutes

later they came back with water and lifted it to my mouth. "Here, drink some of this, it'll help."

I managed a few sips and Michael said, "Let's get you walking a bit." He pulled me up with help from someone else and, with my arms over their shoulders, they walked me up and down.

"He's had water and he's moving. The house is full of booze. I don't know."

"What else have you had?"

I nodded and groaned.

"What have you had?"

I pulled at my pocket.

They kept putting the glass of water up to my lips every couple of minutes and pushing me to walk.

"I've found a pink tablet."

"It's not medicine. It's big and grainy."

I could hear sirens.

"Yes, they're here now."

The sirens got closer and closer, until an ambulance drove up the driveway and the crew got out. I was put back down onto the bench and sat upright. Two men came and knelt in front of me. One put a blood pressure cuff on my arm and started pumping it. The other pulled open my eyes and shone a light in them.

"Andy, listen, I'm here to help. Can you tell me what you've taken?"

Michael handed him the pink pill.

"Andy, look at me," the paramedic said, and I opened my eyes. "How many of these have you had?"

I held up two fingers.

"And how much have you drunk?"

I couldn't speak.

"The house is full of it," Michael said.

"Andy, listen, I want you to stand up and take a few steps."

He pulled me up and got me walking with an arm around

my waist. My eyes were now partly open and I could see things in a blur.

"That's great. Now can you drink a glass of water for me?" he said, and passed me the glass.

I drank it, sip by sip, until it was gone.

"Excellent. You're gonna be fine." He sat me upright on the bench again and stood up to talk to Michael.

"Can someone stay with him?" he said, and Michael nodded. "Any problems at all, call us. If he passes out or starts vomiting, call us."

After the ambulance had gone, I sat on the back step drinking a glass of water and a girl sat with me and held my hand. People were filtering in and out of the rooms and garden, and I found it comforting. They were all there for me. The group of young people all knew each other from church, where Michael was still the youth leader. I didn't know half of them. It had been years since I'd last been to church.

As it got later, people started leaving and Michael said, "You should get some sleep."

"Thanks for… you know," I said, and he waved it away like it was nothing.

"Is there a bed I can use?" he said. I led him to the spare room and pulled out clean sheets.

"I'm up at six, but wake me if you need anything." He put a hand on my shoulder. "Get some sleep. I'll pray for you."

I got into bed feeling safe and secure.

But as soon as I fell asleep, I saw myself falling face-first into water and sinking down, down, down into the depth beneath me. I kept sinking, sinking, sinking, lower and lower and lower. The cold turned my body numb. I sank lower and lower. I was scared. I swung my arms around, but couldn't swim. I breathed and my lungs filled with water. My body went still and all I could do was look above. But I could see nothing except blackness.

I slept through until late morning, except for a brief

moment when Michael woke me with a soft hand on my back as he was leaving. He said, "Don't forget, he's always there for you, wherever you go."

7

Lee Lane joined the village where I lived with the next one along. A sixty mile per hour road without a footpath that bent around corners and rose to blind summits. Unlit and with dense bushes and trees along the sides, it was a mile of dark and dangerous road.

I'd been at Jim's all night smoking pot, drinking and listening to music. A friend of his was there too. His name was Mark, but Jim called him Mouse with regard to his small stature and protruding ears. When it got to three in the morning, Mouse decided to walk home and no amount of cajoling would convince him otherwise. He lived in the next village, so his journey would take him up Lee Lane. Once Mouse had left, we thought no more about it and got some sleep. In the morning, I left.

I returned to Jim's a few hours later and knocked on the door.

Jim opened it. His eyes were red and swollen. "Mouse is dead."

I was dreaming about being in a fight. I couldn't see my opponent, but he was hitting me. I couldn't block his punches. All I could do was duck and move around. Then when I tried to hit him, my fist found air. So I tried to kick him, but my leg wouldn't move. I swung my hips trying to get my leg up, but it was stuck to the floor. The punches and kicks rained down on me and I spun around trying to dodge them.

Then I woke up covered in sweat and kicking my covers. There was pressure in my chest and I couldn't get enough air. I reached for my inhaler and took several puffs. I put my head in my hands. At the side of the bed was a bottle of whisky. I grabbed it and took a few deep gulps, then lit a cigarette. But I still felt anxious. I needed something else. Downstairs, I routed through the medicine cupboard looking for codeine, sleeping tablets or anything to get relief. There was nothing good. So I took a pill out of every bottle, blister and box and laid them out on the side. There was everything from antibiotics to dog worming tablets. I slid them off the counter into my palm, took a breath, and then swallowed the lot with a slug of whisky.

I sat down on the couch and waited.

You don't wanna do this.

After ten minutes, I had to get them out, so I went and drank a pint of salt water and sprayed the sink with the coloured pills. I finished the booze and smoked and smoked, but the pressure was still there. Sweat dripped from my head. I went to the bathroom and took a plastic razor and broke it open. I sat on the edge of the bath and made a couple of shallow cuts on my forearm. Blood grew from them in tiny red orbs, beading along the lines of the wounds. My breathing slowed. I cut again, and again, just small, surface cuts in a straight line. My body relaxed. There was no pain, just a scraping feeling across the skin. I pushed my finger into the blood and smoothed it across the wounds. It felt warm and comforting. I lifted my arm to my mouth and cleaned my skin. Something had released in my stomach and now my heartbeat was steady and my breathing calm.

I thought about my mum. She hadn't been sleeping well. She would always be awake whatever time of night I got in. It was my fault. I knew that. The doctor had put her on sleeping pills, but she didn't want to take them. I thought about those pills, hiding somewhere in the house. Sitting in a dark cupboard or drawer, waiting to be found. I got up and started in the bathroom cabinet.

They have to be somewhere.

I heard the front door open and my parents come in.

"Wish I could nap all day, but some of us have to work," my mum said.

A small corner of my mind was still operating, telling me what was happening. The rest of me was a lump of useless flesh, shaking and unconscious on the couch. I heard the sounds of shoes being removed, coats hung up, and footsteps across carpet, then wood. I could hear them standing, staring, looking at me and not moving. I felt it. I heard it louder than all the other sounds put together.

They sat down and the television came to life.

"Tea?" my dad said, and went to put the kettle on. He came back in and asked me if I wanted one, but I couldn't answer. He shook me, but I didn't stir. I couldn't move. I was in limbo. I could still hear and sense the outside world, but it was fading. In my bubble, I could see another world of churning black shapes at the back of my eyes.

He felt my forehead and called my mum. "I can't wake him. He's soaked with sweat," he said.

They were stood over me, staring at me again, but I couldn't speak. My mum listened for my breathing and checked my pulse. She touched my head and pulled up my eyelids.

"What's wrong with him?" my dad said, while pacing up and down.

The couch had me sucked into its bowels, again. It was always my last refuge when things went too far. I crawled onto it when I needed to be found.

My mum was looking through my pockets, emptying cigarettes, lighter, and money onto the side. She knew what had happened. She looked under the couch and in my coat. I heard the sound of cardboard and the metallic scrape of empty strips of tablets being pulled out.

"He's taken the lot," she said.

Screaming faces lunged at me and engulfed my head. I wanted to scream. I wanted to jump up and out of the mess I was in. But I was bound and gagged, weighed down and dropped into deep, black water. I could feel my legs twitching, but could do nothing. Now they knew. Now they could help.

"He's so pale. Let's call an ambulance," my dad said.

My mum sighed. "He'll be fine. He got himself into this mess, he can ride it out."

My lungs were full of the blackness and it had turned my eyes dark. I'd sunk to a wet hell of silt and sludge. Starved of oxygen and a hundred leagues from life. I was drowning. I imagined my death under water, unable to breathe.

I could just about hear my mum crying. She was sat at the end of the couch next to my legs. She laid her hand on my back and said, "I'll call Dr Wood."

The next day everything started the same way, maybe worse. Pressure in my chest, my temples thumping, sweating into my clothes even though I was cold. I couldn't stay still. I needed to get out of the house.

My mum was sat in the lounge. "Where you going?" she said.

"Out." I pulled on my shoes.

She stood up. "Where?"

"Why do you wanna know?"

"I need to know you're safe." She came towards me and took my hand. "We love you."

I looked away. I wanted to run away. "I'm fine. I'll be

back later." A tear rolled down my cheek, but I didn't know what I was feeling, so I pulled my hand out of hers and opened the door.

"What happened yesterday?" she said.

I stopped. "I dunno," I said, "I just…"

"I've asked Dr Wood to have a chat with you."

I clenched my fists. *What for? It was a mistake.* I walked out and down the street. I knew she was watching me, as I didn't hear the door close, but I didn't turn around. I kept walking until I knew she couldn't see me.

I felt better when I walked as fast as I could through the cold air. I lit a cigarette. The pressure was still there in my chest, but I knew what to do. I pulled the coins from my pocket and counted them. There wasn't enough for anything good, so I bought the biggest bottle of white cider that I could afford and headed to Jim's.

When he saw the cider he said, "Times must be hard."

I laughed. "Need to get wasted today."

"Bong?" he said.

I shook my head. "That stuff just makes me happy."

Jim started to set it up for himself. "That's why I love it," he said.

I couldn't relax. I poured a pint of the cider out and downed it. The chemical taste made my mouth water and go loose, but I managed to hold it down. I poured another and downed it. I lit a cigarette to stop the gagging sensation in my throat. I didn't want to be sick. I poured out another glass and the bottle was over half way down already.

"Steady on, fella, you'll be trolleyed."

I drained the glass. "That's the idea."

"How's that gonna help?"

I shrugged, "Maybe it'll kill me."

He wrinkled his brow and shook his head. "Maybe you should talk to someone," he said, and I felt like punching him.

Who the hell is he to lecture me?

I downed two more glasses and the bottle was nearly empty. I got up and went to the toilet. I walked into the door and scraped along the wall. I missed the toilet and it was all over the floor, the wall, and on my jeans. I went back into the bedroom and fell, knocking the bong bucket over. Five litres of stinking, dirty bong water spread across the carpet and then vanished beneath it.

"Idiot! Get a towel," Jim said, but he looked at me and shook his head and went for the towel himself. "Are you helping, or what?"

"Sorry, man," I said, "sorry." I picked up my bottle and went downstairs to leave. I bounced off every wall and door frame as I made my way through to the front door.

Jim came after me. "Wait, have a coffee," he said, and pulled me into the kitchen.

I leant back on the counter and tried to get my head to stay still, so the room wouldn't spin so much.

"Give me this," Jim said, and tried to take my cider.

I pulled away and put it to my lips and gulped the last few inches down.

He watched.

"You'll kill yourself with that."

"I wanna die anyway," I said, "watch." I picked up a knife off the side and ran it across my wrist. I thought I'd only done it gently, but my skin split open and for a brief moment I could see tendons, pink flesh and white bone before the wound filled with dark blood.

Jim went white and held onto the side, as blood dripped onto the floor in thick blobs. He grabbed a towel and wrapped it around my wrist, but the blood seeped through.

"I'm calling an ambulance."

I shook my head and went for the door.

Jim stood in my way, but I pushed past him and walked out. He called after me, but I ignored him.

My vision was blurred and the street in front of me was moving around. I kept looking down at my wrist and the towel that was filling with blood. I ran, but fell over into a hedge. I got up and kept going, staying near hedges and walls. When I got home, I sat in the garden and lit a cigarette. It got covered in bloody finger prints, but I smoked it anyway. I felt my stomach churn, and moved ready for it. I threw up over the floor between my legs. Hot, fizzy, steaming cider drenched the floor and my shoes. It stunk of acid.

I heard the back door open and my mum's voice, "What's happened? You're bleeding."

It was too late to hide. She was already coming up the garden. I turned away, but she came and grabbed my arm and pulled off the towel. "Hospital, no arguments."

I shook my head and put the towel back around my wrist.

"Get in the car."

"You don't care about me." I got up and walked out of the garden. I got down the driveway before throwing up again, covering the wall. She went into the house. I felt weak, so sat down against the wall and closed my eyes. The pressure in my chest felt better – the chaos, the alcohol, the blood, and the panic had helped. I lit another cigarette, leant back and smoked. I got back to the bench in the garden and lay down. There was less spinning with my eyes closed. I tucked my legs up and held my bloodied arm with my other hand and rested.

Then Dr Wood was stood over me. "What's he's been doing now?" He was looking at me, but addressing my mum.

"Do you want to tell me about it?"

I sat up. I shrugged. I tried to look sober. "I cut my wrist."

His eyes narrowed and the hand on his leather bag gripped tighter. "Okay, let's go inside and take a look."

On the dining room table, he unwrapped my arm and raised his eyebrows. "Uh-huh." He put his glasses onto the end of his nose, washed my wound and laid my arm onto a clean towel. Blood was still seeping from it, but not as much as before.

"Will this hurt?" I said. I could feel stinging and I knew

the alcohol was wearing off.

"I've no anaesthetic, so you'll have to grin and bear it."

There was more tugging and pulling than pain, and when I looked down I just saw a piece of meat being trussed up.

"How did it happen?" he said, not looking up from his sewing.

"I fell on some glass."

He continued stitching the wound, then cleaned and bandaged it. I thanked him and went outside for a cigarette. As he was leaving, he popped back out into the garden and said, "Your mum says you've been struggling lately and I wondered if we could have a chat about it."

I shrugged and took a drag on my cigarette.

He smiled. Then left.

I took out another cigarette and lit it with the last. *Maybe it won't be so bad if he can help me with the pressure in my chest. He could help me feel calmer.* I felt better, but tired. I finished my cigarette and went to go to bed, but as I walked inside I saw Michael sat in the living room. He smiled and waved me over to the couch.

"Can we have a chat?"

I wanted to say *no, you're the last person I want to talk to,* but I owed him five minutes after what he did for me last time. I walked over to the chair near the window and sat there instead of the couch. I wanted to leave, but I knew he meant well.

"How's life treating you?"

Are you insane? I've just cut open my wrist with a kitchen knife. I drink every day and take any drug I can get my hands on. What do you think?

"Fine," I said, as my back started to sweat.

"Things could be better, though?" He kept smiling the whole way through the sentence.

You're a psychopath. Of course, things could be better. I could be dead and not speaking to you.

I shrugged. "Maybe."

"I've been praying for you," he said, trying to keep eye contact. "Have you thought about church?"

I tried to form a reply, but couldn't think what to say except *no, no, no, no no, never never never,* so I just smiled.

"Hey, no pressure," he held up his hand. "Just think about it, okay?"

I tried another smile and waited for him to leave.

"Is there anything you want to ask me?"

No, we're done here. Why does everyone want to talk?

I shook my head.

"Are you shutting me out?"

"I'm just tired."

"You know where to find me if you want to talk." He stood up, but instead of leaving he came over to me and knelt down. "Can I pray for you?" he said, but before I could answer, he put his hand on my shoulder and closed his eyes. "Lord, I ask that you'll be with Andy now and that you'll watch over him, bless him and keep him safe wherever he goes and whatever he does. Amen." I mouthed amen when he finished, as he was looking right at me.

It wasn't too bad, but I still felt like wriggling away. I preferred being stitched up without anaesthetic. I didn't want praying for and I didn't want God coming with me to watch what I got up to either. He wouldn't want to see what I got up to. He wouldn't like it at all.

I knew I was dreaming. I was stood at the bow of a boat, surveying the ocean stretching out before me. The water was calm and blue and reflected the clear sky. In an instant, it turned grey. The waves began to grow making the boat bob and rock. I held on, but the waves got bigger and more violent. I lost balance and fell overboard. I expected to hit water and go under, but I kept falling and falling through the air, faster and faster. When I did land, I hit the springs in my mattress and bounced myself awake. The thud of my heart beating was all I could hear. It was morning and the sun glowed behind the curtains.

My bedroom door opened. "Don't forget your appointment with Dr Wood," my mum said, picking up dirty clothes from my floor.

I groaned and rolled onto my side, pulling the covers over my head to block the light.

"It's in half an hour, so I suggest you get ready."

At the surgery, I sat in the waiting room hoping no one could see how hungover and grey I was. My heart was pounding and I felt the pressure in my chest again. I wiped away sweat from my forehead and hid my shaking by jigging my leg up and down.

As I poked my face around his door, he smiled and said, "Come in, come sit down." I sat beside his desk and he leant back on his swivel chair. "How you doing?"

I don't want to be alive.

"Fine." I said, and a cold bead of sweat ran down the middle of my back.

"I understand you've been down and drinking heavily."

I looked at the floor and back at him. I shrugged. My hands found the ends of the chair arms and gripped them.

"Do you think you're depressed?" He interlaced his fingers and rested them in his lap.

I stared at the wall. *I think I need a drink.*

He sighed and sat up. "The last time I saw you, you'd had that *accident*. What happened?"

I pulled myself up in the chair. "It was nothing. Just stress."

Just tell me what's wrong and how to fix it.

"Do you feel like that today?"

I'm getting close.

"A little," I said, squeezing the chair arms.

"Can you describe your feelings?"

I feel like I want to get out of this room. I feel like I want a drink. I feel pressure in my chest that makes me want to swallow a box of pills and hit myself in the head. I feel like everything is flat, colourless and

102

plain except my mind that's thinking ten thoughts a second and won't be quiet and I wish I could unplug it.

"Frustrated," I said.

He smiled and nodded, but I knew he had no idea. He sat looking at me. His gold glasses were shining against his tanned skin.

How can you ever understand?

"Okay, this is a tough one, but do you ever feel like you want to end your life?"

I thought for a few seconds. *Sometimes I don't want to live and I wonder what the point of my life is. I wonder what the point of everything is.*

I shook my head.

He lifted his right hand up to his chin and held it. His gaze shifted from me to the desk and back. The pressure in my chest got worse and I felt like I'd said too much. I started to sweat more, down my back and under my arms. There was a noise. A clunk clunk clunk that didn't stop. I looked around for the source. There was a clock on the far wall near the examination table. A slow seconds hand was thumping out the rhythm. I stared at it and it seemed to slow. Each second dragged by. A minute took an hour. In the background the sounds of the surgery echoed around my head. Then a new sound of tap taptaptap tap tap started, and I looked around to see Dr Wood typing on his computer and mouthing something. I refocused my attention and heard the end of what he was saying.

"...so we'll start you on 20mg of Cipramil a day and see how you get on. Okay?"

I stared at him trying to focus my mind on what he was saying.

"It'll be a week before you notice a change, but give me a call if you still feel the same."

He handed me the prescription and smiled.

"Is that it?" I said.

"Yes, that's everything. Give it a go for a week and see

how you feel."

I woke in a haze. Not the usual hangover fog, but a heavy veil that dampened sight and sound. The usual pressure in my chest was there, but even that was dulled. The riot of thoughts that usually spun around my head were quiet, but a shadow hung over me that I'd not felt before. A darkness at my core, a weight in my stomach, a low rumble in my guts.

I bought a four pack of beer and a bottle of cooking brandy. I started drinking the beers on the way home from the shop. The taste made me feel better. The alcohol flicked a switch in my body that said, *everything will be fine now*. The thrill of getting booze made me walk with purpose and I was back in minutes. I sat in the living room and drank and smoked. I didn't think or feel. I just did. The wrinkles in my forehead flattened and my back loosened as I drank more. But the weight in my stomach still dragged me down. I was going to get wasted no matter what.

I kept drinking and smoking, but I couldn't get enough. I drank all the beers and walked up and down the living room. I couldn't shake the overwhelming sense of dread. I went to the couch and tried to sleep, but felt my heart beating in my throat. I needed it to be quiet. I needed to slow it down. I needed some pills. In a bag stuffed to the back of a drawer, was my mum's medication. I pulled out a strip of the codeine and took six with a gulp of brandy and pocketed the rest with four Zimovane for later.

The warm, cosy feeling grew from my feet up and I basked in it. Comfort and warmth blanketed my back and I swigged the brandy and smoked. I couldn't stay at that level, though. Once I started, I had to keep going until I lost myself. I needed more. Always more. So I drank. I smoked. I took codeine. I kept repeating the pattern until it was early evening, then left the house. I wanted to be gone by the time my parents got back from work.

I sat in the park and finished the bottle of brandy and the

codeine. It was winter, but I was wearing only my jeans and a T-shirt. I couldn't feel the cold. I lit a cigarette and headed to the pub.

It was two-for-one on spirits, so I ordered a quadruple gin with ice. I sat at the bar and drank my booze, hoping no one would talk to me. I lit a cigarette and ordered another quad gin. The barmaid paused and looked at me for a minute, but then made the drink. I ignored her and looked at the bottles behind the bar, moving my head from side to side. The bottles moved around and bounced up and down. I slipped off my stool and headed to the toilet. Everything was bouncing before my eyes – the red carpet, the wooden furniture, the shiny brass bar. I made my way there by hanging onto the backs of chairs for support.

When I got back to my seat, I ordered the same again, but that time the barmaid hesitated. She put her hand on her hip and said, "Last one, okay?" She put the gin down and I picked it up and downed it.

"Another," I said, and held the glass towards her.

She shook her head and turned away, then went to serve someone at the other end of the bar.

I stumbled off my stool and got ready to leave. I picked up the glass and threw it at the bar. It shattered, and pieces spread across the wooden top and down onto the floor. I turned to leave, as a couple of guys stepped off their stools and shouted after me.

It was dark and cars were going past in streaks of blurred light and sound. I stumbled into the road and heard horns get loud then die out. I found the pavement again and watched my feet walk one step at a time. I ended up at the shop standing in front of the booze shelf trying to read bottles, but nothing would hold still. I stuck my hand out to grab something, but there was nothing there. I took a step and tried again. I felt something and tried to grab it. I heard the chink of glass bottles, but I couldn't grip them.

"Looks like you've had enough already." A guy was stood

next to me. He smiled.

I shook my head and he laughed.

"What you after?"

"Thunderbird."

He handed me a bottle.

I walked to the bus shelter and sat down. I opened the bottle and took a long drink. I lit a cigarette and leaned back. There was still no overthinking in my mind and the pressure in my chest hadn't returned. But in my stomach, the clot was there. The heavy weight of guilt, or fear, or something, was sat in my gut and wouldn't go. I tried to drown it with booze and soften it with codeine, but it persisted. Then I remembered the Zimovane in my pocket. I pulled them out and swallowed them. Nothing can beat oblivion. I wanted all my feelings to go. I wanted to be numb. I wanted to be unconscious. I got to my feet and started walking again. I drank. I walked. I smoked. I walked and drank until the streetlights ran out and the bottle was empty.

I was stood at the bottom of Lee Lane. It curved round in front of me. A dark tunnel of a road with thick skeletal bushes on either side. I started to walk along the road, leaving the lights of the village behind me and going further into the darkness.

As I passed the first corner, I felt the quiet of the dark and deserted place. My body was beginning to feel limp. My eyelids were heavy and I couldn't keep them open. I walked a little further until I felt too tired to go on. I wanted to sleep. I was free of the pressure and pain and panic, but I needed to rest. I looked for a place to sit. At the side of the road, I shuffled next to the hedges and leant back. I thought I was safe, but I was still on the road. My head lolled forward and I couldn't keep it up. I lay back onto the ground and stretched out my legs. Cars were swerving past me, but I thought they were nowhere near me. It started to snow.

I looked up into the sky and watched the flakes float down onto my face. I closed my eyes. Peace. Quiet. Calm. I opened them again and everything was beautiful. The snow looked white and clean. It was quiet. I felt calm. The pressure in my chest was gone. The weight in my stomach was gone. My mind was silent. I felt nothing. I was numb. I was free.

I let myself relax. I let myself sleep. I let myself go.

8

I lay there unconscious, unmoving. The snow fell heavier and heavier, blanketing the ground, hiding my body. With the snow, came stillness and quiet. The temperature fell and the snowflakes grew larger, filling the sky. Passing cars got closer and closer, seeing my body only seconds before swerving out of the way. None of them stopped. Not one driver got out to help. But then two men started to walk towards the road and around the corner. They put up their hands to stop the traffic, as they picked me up off the road. Both of them took an arm around their shoulders and dragged me from Lee Lane to the other side of the road and made their way towards my estate. They carried me up my street and directly to my house. They knocked on the front door and were greeted by my mum.

"Is that Andy? What's happened?" my mum said.

They smiled, nodded, but didn't speak. My mum stepped aside for them to come in and they laid me on the couch. She covered me in a blanket and checked I was breathing.

"Where was he?" my mum said, but they were already outside the door.

They stopped and turned around. "Lee Lane. Cars were

swerving around him," one of them said, then they turned and walked down the street.

"How did you know where he lived?" my mum said, but they carried on walking until they were out of sight.

I woke up on the couch fully dressed. I even had my shoes on. The house was almost silent, but I could sense someone. I opened my eyes to see my parents stood over me.

"You're lucky you can open your eyes this morning. You should be dead," my dad said.

My mum cried and touched my head.

My dad hugged her. "You're making your mother ill. It has to stop," he said.

I stared at them. My head was pounding. My mouth was dry. My memory blank. I searched for fragments from the day before. *Booze, pills, pub, but then what?*

"What happened?" I said. My voice was gravel.

"You got blind drunk and decided to sleep in the road."

I sat up and rubbed my eyes. "How did I get home?"

"Two blokes carried you," my dad said.

My mum sat down beside me and held my hand. "Any longer and you'd have got hypothermia."

I looked at my mum and wanted to cry. I squeezed her hand and smiled. "Sorry," I said.

My dad stood with his hands on his hips. "We won't watch you kill yourself."

My mum took my hand in both of hers and looked at me. "I don't want to worry anymore."

I looked at both of them. I could see love, but also exhaustion. I knew I had to go.

I ignored the pressure in my chest and the blood thumping through the arteries in my throat. I grabbed a rucksack and stuffed clothes and toiletries into it. I took my bankcard and a coat. I Bought cigarettes and whisky and started walking. I didn't need anything else. I kept walking and walking, but didn't even get out of the village. I walked through the streets and around the park. Down through the ginnels and near the dike. Along the canal and onto the old railway lines. I circled the village several times. Thinking. Thinking. Thinking. With every step, I said, *where should I go? Where should I go? Where should I go?*

And then I stopped walking. I had to sit down. I looked up and saw that I was next to the football field near where my grandma and grandad used to live. To my left was the cemetery. I walked in and went to their graves. I sat facing them. *I wish you were here.* I put my head in my hands and sobbed. I drank. I cried. I smoked.

I tried to breathe, but I was suffocating. I was trapped. In the village, in my life, in my mind and in my body. I had to get away. I had to find some space to figure things out. I went back home and to the small booklet that had taken me to Texas. I scoured the pages – ski resorts in France, Kibbutz in Israel, teaching English in Japan – but it all felt too much. Then a leaflet fell out of the back. It said, *Escape the office and the grind of 9-5, work for the YHA this summer.*

I saw ESCAPE in large letters and picked up the phone. I told them I wanted to leave as soon as possible and they set me up with a telephone interview. They put me through to Dave who managed a hostel down south. Someone had just left and there was a job. I told him I'd be there in a few days. He was friendly and happy to have someone so eager.

The night before I left, Jim got some speed. A big ball of sticky yellow base, which we shared between us and stayed up all night rattling around his house.

I was coming down as I got home, and slipped into the shower just before my parents got up. My skin prickled and I shivered. As I walked across the landing, I could hear them talking in their bedroom. My dad sounded positive and thought the responsibility to look after myself would be good, but my mum was crying. Between the tears I heard her say, "We might not see him alive again."

I pulled my door shut without a sound and sat on the bed. At first I thought it was an overreaction, but the thoughts echoed around my head. *Could I die? Will I die?* Then I felt sick in the bottom of my stomach, a crippling cramp that made me bend over and clench my fists. I closed my eyes and tensed my body. Then it was gone, as quick as it had started. I lit a cigarette and sat at the window.

The familiar structure of the gasometer met us as we approached Barnsley. We climbed up Eldon Street between stone terraced houses and under the railway bridge. As we pulled into the bus station, busses swung around onto the road heading out of town. We parked at the side and pulled our coats around our necks. We pushed through the biting wind towards the concrete island where the coach was waiting.

My eyes watered with the cold and my back stiffened. I pulled out a cigarette and smoked it in silence. My parents smiled at me and walked on the spot to keep warm. They sucked air through their teeth and pulled their shoulders up to keep out the cold.

I racked my brain for something to say, but I had nothing. I wanted to say that I *would* come back alive, that she had just been paranoid. But I wasn't sure. It wasn't like my mum to exaggerate. When I turned to her, she was looking at me. Her eyes were red with a far-off stare. I wanted to get away. I wanted some space. But I felt stuck to the spot. I felt like I couldn't leave. *Is this the last time I'll see them?*

I threw my rucksack into the luggage compartment and turned back to my parents. "I've got to go," I said, and forced a smile.

"We love you," my mum said, and hugged me. Her voice was shaky.

My dad came over and joined in on the hug, rubbing my back with his hand. "If you need anything, just give us a ring," he said.

My mum held me for a little longer. "We'll always love you no matter what," she said, and squeezed my hand.

"I'm only going for the summer," I said.

She went to speak, but stopped. She wiped her eyes and attempted a smile. "Don't forget where we are if you need us," she said, forcing a last smile.

I walked up the steps and turned to wave. They were hugging and my mum had her face in my dad's shoulder. He waved back, but she didn't look. I headed to the back of the bus.

I slept for the whole journey, waking just in time to see the coach pass by Swanage seafront. Even in the grey February light, the view was beautiful. At the top of a very steep hill was the hostel, a grand Victorian building with a heavy oak door. I rang the bell at the desk and a grey-haired man came through.

"Can I help?"

"Hi, I'm Andy, I—"

"Oh, of course, come on through, we're just serving dinner," he said, opening the hatch. "I'm Dave."

He led me into the kitchen where several people were busy mopping, washing dishes, and putting pans away. Dave started pointing at people. "My wife Tracy, Lee over there, Marie washing up, and Drew and Beccy stacking chairs," but I couldn't take it all in. I stood looking around at them feeling my face beginning to flush.

"I'll show you your room, so you can unpack," he said, and took me out of the back door and up to an annex. "This is where you and the guys live. Me and Tracy are over there in the bungalow." He pointed at the house next door, then left.

The room was basic and the windows looked out to a densely wooded and unkempt no man's land behind the annex, which made the room dark. But it also felt secluded and private. I leant my rucksack in the corner, lit a cigarette and sat on the bed. All I could think about was getting a

112

drink, so I grabbed my coat and headed out.

As I left the room, I bumped into one of the guys.

"Hi mate, I'm Lee." He held out his hand and I shook it. "Could murder a few beers," he said, sucking on a roll up, "wanna grab a pint?"

We walked back down past the kitchen. "Should we invite the others?" I said.

Lee shook his head. "Nar, Marie is off to meet her new boyfriend and Drew and Beccy are boring."

I lit a cigarette and offered one to Lee.

"Safe," he said, and lit it.

I tried to keep up with Lee, but he was much taller than me and took huge strides, which made his baggy jeans flap in the wind. We went to The Ship at the bottom of the street and Lee went up to the bar. I got us a table. The pub was decorated like its name suggested with wooden floors and ropes, rigging, and lifebuoys hanging from the walls and ceiling.

After a few pints, we were both laughing and getting along when Lee said, "Mate, your pupils are huge."

"Must be the beer," I said.

He laughed. "Look in the mirror."

I stood up and looked in a mirror on the wall. The black of my pupils had taken over and left only a ring of blue. I sat back down and felt a tingle slide through my body.

Wow, I'm back up, I thought.

"Had a bit of marching powder or something?" Lee said, rubbing a hand over his shaved head.

It was too late to lie, so I shrugged and smiled, "Had some speed last night."

"Safe, I've got someone to share a joint with now."

I laughed. "You got any on you?"

"No, but," he looked over his shoulder and bent closer to me, lowering his voice, "there's a dealer in here. Over on the other side of the bar."

I looked over to the other side and there were quite a few

people milling around, talking and drinking.

"The guy with dreadlocks. Can't miss him," he said.

Lee went to get some drinks and to catch his eye. He walked around the bar and had a brief chat with him. Then came and sat back down. "What brought you down here, anyway?" Lee said.

I felt my chest tighten and the blood thud in my neck. *Why am I here?* I looked out of the window and tried to think what to say. Then I looked back at him and he was smiling and the panic went. "Just needed a break from boring jobs and that."

Lee smiled and nodded. We both took a drink of our pints.

"You?"

"Saving up to travel round Thailand."

Just then the dealer came over to us and sat down. He nodded at Lee, then looked at me and waited.

"Jay, Andy. Andy, Jay," Lee said.

Jay then nodded at me. He turned to Lee and said, "Twenty-five."

Lee took some money out and handed it over and Jay passed him a bag of weed. Then Jay stood up and said, "Lee. Andy." Then nodded and left.

We finished our drinks and headed back up the hill to the hostel, stopping at the off-license on the way. Back in the annex, we opened a bottle of wine and went into the garden and Lee rolled a couple of joints. It was night, but we sat out on the white patio furniture moving every few minutes so that the security light stayed on.

"What's everyone else like?" I said.

"Marie's a top lass, but Drew and Beccy don't like anyone," Lee said, and sucked on his joint.

The next morning, I woke up late. Everyone else was cleaning the hostel for a group arriving at the end of the week. I wasn't due to start work for another day, so I headed down into the town. It was cold and quiet. Every other shop was shut and only a handful of people were walking through the streets. I made my way along the road next to the shore and sat on a grass verge looking out to sea. There was an ice-cream parlour and a rock shop to one side, both boarded up and dark. Their red and white painted signs looking out of place next to the grey sky.

I bought a bottle of whisky and took it down to the beach. I walked along the edge of the water from one side to the other, where the sea nibbled at the cliffs, then scrambled over the rocks as far as I could. I found a spot nestled in against the overhang with views all around. Leaning against the rock sheltered me from the sea breeze and I felt warm and calm. The pressure in my chest had subsided since arriving in Swanage and I liked the change of scene. It was hard not to feel lifted by the sea view, the lapping of the water and birds surfing the wind, but I couldn't ignore that ever-present ache deep in my stomach.

I watched the boats bob across the line where the sea meets the sky, and tried to think of nothing. But my parents came into mind. I could feel my back prickle, as I thought of my mum and what she'd said. I drank and smoked and pushed the thoughts away. I watched the water and let myself relax and breathe the cool fresh air. *Everything will be okay,* I thought, but tears ran down my cheeks and fell off my chin. I cried about nothing and everything. I cried because maybe she was right.

I cried because now I was alone.

9

As soon as I woke up that morning, I drank some leftover wine and smoked a couple of cigarettes while still in bed. I brushed my teeth, spitting out the blood from my bleeding gums. Then I threw up. This had become my daily routine.

It was my twenty first birthday and I'd booked a few days off to go home and see my parents. I packed a small rucksack and headed out to catch my coach. As I passed the hostel kitchen, Tracy saw me and called me inside. It was just before the breakfast was to be served and everyone was in the kitchen preparing food. I walked in and looked around at them and tried to smile, but something didn't feel right. They stopped what they were doing and came and stood around looking at me.

Tracy went into the office and brought out a bag. "Happy twenty first," she said, and handed it to me. Inside was a bottle of champagne. I didn't know what to say. I hadn't told anyone it was my birthday.

I stood there as each person hugged me, gave me their best wishes, then handed me a gift. It wasn't what I expected or what I wanted. If it wasn't for the wine, I would have been angry. I left with four bottles weighing my bag down. As I walked, I felt a heavier burden in my stomach. That tight knot of guilt and fear. I didn't want to go home. I didn't want to see my parents. But I'd promised them I was coming. My chest tightened and I felt the blood thudding in my neck.

As the coach pulled into London, the driver came on the tannoy and said there would be a two-hour wait before the journey continued to Barnsley. I felt relieved and excited. I got off the coach and headed up the street towards Hyde Park. On the way, I bought a corkscrew from a gift shop. Then I found a quiet spot under a tree to drink. I opened the first bottle and gulped half of it down in one and said to myself, *just one bottle, it will help*. I kept gulping it down and saying to myself, *you have to go, you have to go*. But I didn't want to see my parents, or my home. The pressure in my chest started to suffocate me. I lit a cigarette and felt calmer. I lay back on the grass and blew the smoke up towards the leaves. *Another bottle wouldn't hurt,* I told myself, as I pulled one out of my bag.

I took that bottle slower and tried to enjoy the flavour. But then I thought of what my mum and dad would say if I walked off the coach drunk. They'd expect it, but they'd still be disappointed. That would make me feel worse and then I'd drink more and things would fall apart.

Home is a black hole and I'm not going to walk into it.

All around me people walked hand in hand, or cycled, or sat in groups eating picnics and talking and laughing. Dogs ran and barked with their tongues lolling out of their mouths. But I sat in the shade and I drank and smoked.

I finished the second bottle and looked at the time – the coach was leaving in thirty minutes. I got up and started to walk. The thudding in my chest was audible and my breathing was fast and shallow. I couldn't see the way I'd come in, so kept walking one way then the next and then the next until I found it.

Twenty minutes left.

I'm not going home. There's nothing there for me.

I swung my bag on my back and jogged towards the station. My lungs hurt and my head spun. I felt that I might trip and fall at any moment, so I slowed down to a walk.

Ten minutes.

What am I doing? I don't want to see them.

I reached the station with only two minutes to spare but stopped in the entrance and leant on the wall. I could see my coach and the driver. He was shutting the storage space underneath, ready to set off. I watched and said out loud, "I'm not going. I'm not going," as I circled the pavement and kicked the wall. I fought off the urge to run to the coach. I lit a cigarette and counted the thuds in my chest. The coach passed me on the way out. As it slipped past the corner, the weight in my stomach lifted and I felt better. I headed back to the park to continue drinking.

The champagne was warm, but I opened it anyway. "Happy twenty first to me," I said, and took a gulp.

I don't care if I'm twenty-one. It means nothing to me.

I gulped the wine and smoked. I pushed the thoughts of home and my parents away.

This is exactly what I want to do.
This is exactly where I want to be.
I don't need anyone or anything else.

Someone arranged a staff night out. It wasn't my idea of fun, but I felt obliged to go. I made sure I was drunk by the time I got there. We met in a wine bar for a meal, before heading to the other pubs around town. I chose some food and scanned down the wine list to find a bottle of red with the highest alcohol percentage, then ordered it.

It was quiet inside, with just the faint sound of piano music in the background and the lights on low. Everyone talked and laughed and even the tink of cutlery on plates sounded polite and refined. I hated it. My whole body was tense and tingled with energy. I was a stretched elastic band. I wanted to be let loose to cause chaos. I tried to drink my wine like everyone else, but in the end I poured it to the top of the glass and gulped it down.

I was relieved when Dave and Tracy stood up and said, "We're going to say goodnight." That meant we could get drunk.

As soon as the door shut behind them, I said, "Let's go to The Ship." The food was over and the night wasting away. I picked up the remains of my bottle and finished it on the walk over. When we got there, I headed straight to the bar and ordered a pint and a large whisky.

"Steady on," Marie said, "we've got all night."

But Lee ordered the same and winked at me. Marie went to sit with Drew and Beccy, while Lee and I drank at the bar.

"Seen who's over there?" I said, nodding to the far corner where Jay was sat.

Lee looked over and shrugged. "I've got loads of weed left."

"I'm in a party mood," I said, and raised my eyebrows. Lee picked up his pint and took a gulp, then downed his whisky. "I'm fine with booze tonight," he said.

I shrugged. "Be good for the club later."

Lee shook his head. "Can't be bothered with Bar One, it's a dive."

We went over to sit with the others, but I kept an eye on Jay. They were all sat nursing warm beers and looking bored.

"Who's up for Bar One?" I said.

Drew opened his mouth to speak, but Beccy turned to him and narrowed her eyes. He looked down and didn't answer. Marie said she'd come for an hour at the most.

I saw Jay heading towards the side door of the pub, so slipped off to grab him. I followed him out into the street and he turned to look at me.

"Yeah?" he said.

I'd not thought of what to say, so I stood for a minute looking at him. We were under a streetlight, which made it feel seedy.

"If you want something say so, or I'm off." He turned to leave.

I lowered my voice, "Got any speed?"

He shook his head, "Pills. That's it."

"How much?"

"Four for a tenner."

I bought them and had a quick look. They were yellow pills with a smiley face on them. I swallowed one and went back inside.

Drew and Beccy had left and there was just me, Marie and Lee.

"Pints all round?" I said and headed up to the bar. Lee came with me and I held out the pills to show him. I tried to pass him one, but he shook his head.

"I'm not feeling it tonight."

We finished our beers and headed to another bar. The pill had started to kick in and I was feeling hot and excited. The hairs on my legs and arms fizzed. We walked between bars and shouted to one another over the music. I felt like I was sobering up, so suggested shots of tequila and we drank a few together and laughed. I popped to the toilet and took another pill. I stood in front of the floor-to-ceiling mirror looking into the deep black of my pupils, imagining I saw shapes and colours deep inside them. I headed back inside and danced across the dance floor. Marie and Lee mouthed something inaudible to me and I gave them the thumbs up and carried on.

Then I was in Bar One alone. It was so dark, I could see only a hundred red cigarette tips bouncing in front of me and a glowing bar in the distance. Then the music ramped up and fireworks exploded above me. I danced and felt like I was on another planet. The music, the dark, the flashing lights, the humm and fizz of the drugs coursing through my body took me to a place of pure joy.

This can only get better, I thought, so I reached into my pocket and double dropped the remaining two pills.

Within twenty minutes, the fast music warped and slowed and the world around me melted away into abstract colour and shape. My heartbeat thumped in my chest and matched the beat of the music. My chest tightened and I couldn't catch my breath. Spasms hit my stomach and it felt tight and empty. Sounds stuttered in my ears and my eyes could only see blurred images. I stumbled out bumping into shadows flickering in a strobe light. I knew I had to get back to the hostel, so I walked along the high street clinging to the fronts of buildings. I was getting hotter and hotter and needed a drink. I headed to a take away shop and flopped my head onto the counter. "Can I have some water?"

They brought me a glass of water and said, "Drink it and go."

I drank it in big gulps and turned to leave, but my stomach convulsed and I threw up all over the tiled floor.

"Get out, get out." The woman behind the counter came and shooed me away.

Back at the hostel, I knew something was wrong. I fell on my bed crumpled in pain. My stomach churned and groaned and I threw up on the bed sheets and on the floor. I stumbled to the sink and filled it with watery vomit. I tried to look at my face in the mirror, but it was blurred and I couldn't focus. I wanted to ride it out, but I knew I had to get help. Everyone else was in bed and I was too embarrassed to wake them. I went into the hallway, got the phone book and tried to find the number for the Samaritans. The words danced on the page, but I thought I could see the right number, so I called it.

"Samaritans?" I said, my voice thick and slurred.

"No it's not, have you any idea what time it is?" the voice said, so I put the phone down.

The thudding in my chest was so loud it sounded like dance music. I thought it would wake everyone up. I went back into my room and flopped onto the bed. There was a pain in my chest that crushed my ribs and stopped me breathing. I sucked and sucked but only got small breaths. Then my body became rigid and I started to shake. I gripped the bedsheets in my hands and clenched my teeth. I shut my eyes and the room spun. I was terrified.

I had no choice. I rang 999 and asked for an ambulance.

At the hospital, everything was fast and bright. I thought I could still hear music, but it was the rhythmic beeps of heart monitors with the occasional squeak of rubber wheels on hard floors. There were lights everywhere, but they didn't flash like in the club. Instead they seeped their white glow into every orifice and corner of the corridor around me and through my eyes into my body. Everything was illuminated, rather than hidden.

I was wheeled on a bed to a curtained off area and three people stood around me. One put a drip up and threaded a cannula into my arm. Two spoke across me to one another.

"What's he taken?" one said, checking my pulse with two fingers on my wrist.

"Ecstasy." The other pulled up my eyelids and shone a light into them. They looked down and fired questions at me, one after the other.

"Do you know what you've taken?"

"Did you drink with them?"

"How much did you have?"

"Are you a regular drug user?"

I nodded and shook my head and tried to answer, but it was too quick.

Then they both came close and I could see their brows were wrinkled. "This is important, did you take any yellow ecstasy pills?

Yes, but why, why do you want to know? What difference does the colour make?

I nodded.

"Yellow pills?" they said, again.

I nodded.

They looked at each other and raised their eyebrows. They got up close to my face and repeated the question more slowly.

"You're sure they were yellow ecstasy pills?"

I started to nod, as my body went rigid again and I convulsed. My fists were clenched, my teeth were clenched, my whole body was clenched.

"How many did you take?"

"Four," I said, through gritted teeth.

"Nurse!"

Then everything speeded up. People came from all over and surrounded me. They spoke too fast to hear. They moved so quickly that all I saw were floating heads asking me questions.

"You took four yellow pills?"

"Were they yellow pills?"

"Yellow pills?"

"How many yellow pills?"

"Yellow pills. Yellow pills, yellow pills…"

My heart was beating faster and faster and the voices wouldn't stop. My eyes were too wide and letting too much light in. I was cold, so cold that I shivered and I clenched my teeth to stop them chattering. I blinked and blinked to focus more clearly, and curled my toes and stretched my legs, but I was overwhelmed by the surges in my body. I stretched my jaw wide and arched my neck.

My heart was beating saying yel-low, yel-low, yel-low, yel-low yel-low and I wanted to get away or sleep. My eyes rolled back into my head and all I could see was blackness.

The nurse came and drew something up into a syringe and held up her hand and said, "Don't worry, this will help you relax."

I watched the nurse push the needle into the cannula and squeeze. The tightness in my body relented and softened. My legs disappeared, then my waist and stomach. My sight blurred and swam. The heads of the nurses and doctors left their bodies and spun around in circles before my face. Then my chest and arms went and I was just a head on a pillow. I could still hear and think, but my body was gone, sinking into the bed, deep into nothingness. I breathed out one last time and my mind whirred to a stop, my eyelids dropped and I was gone.

When I woke up, I kept my eyes shut for a few minutes. I couldn't remember where I was or how I got there, but I could hear beeps and the rattle of trolleys being wheeled around in the distance. Then I focused in on the sound of soft shoes walking between beds followed by short chitchat. I felt safe, so I opened my eyes. They stung and hurt. I opened my mouth and stretched, but my jaw was stiff and painful. My teeth were on edge. I lifted my head and swallowed. More pain. More stiffness. As I came around, I felt the aching throughout my body. *The hospital, the ecstasy, the ambulance, the club.* It came rushing back to me. I tried to push myself up, but failed and fell back onto the bed.

"Careful," the nurse said, "you've had a rough couple of days."

"Couple of days?"

She stood at the bottom of the bed and pulled out my chart, "You came in the night before last, early hours." She wrapped a blood pressure monitor around my arm and pumped it up. Then she checked my pulse. "That's fine. How are you feeling?"

"Dreadful."

She smiled and jotted some notes on the chart.

I pulled myself up onto my elbows. "When can I go?"

"It won't be today, unless someone can collect you."

As soon as she'd said that, my body went cold, my chest tightened and I breathed short, shallow breaths.

Dave and Tracy are going to find out.

I called the annex hoping Marie would come for me, but there was no answer. I let it ring and ring, but no one was there. *I have to get out of this place. I can't stay here a minute longer.* I took a deep breath and tried the hostel phone.

"Swanage Youth Hostel, Dave speaking."

I froze. *What do I say? How can I get out of this?*

"Hello, can I help?"

My heart raced, thudthudthudthudthud.

"It's Andy."

"What's wrong?"

I messed up, I overdosed, I feel like I've died and come back from hell.

"I'm at Poole hospital. Can you pick me up?"

The line went quiet. I could just hear his breathing. But in that breathing, he was figuring things out. He was coming to terms with it. He knew.

"I'll be there in an hour."

I saw him arrive and come to the door of the ward. He smiled and nodded at me. The nurse went over and they spoke for a few minutes. He nodded and raised his eyebrows and put his hands in his pockets. Then he walked towards me. He walked slower now. The weight of what the nurse had said lying heavy on him. He stood and looked at me. He smiled with one side of his mouth and said, "Come on, we'd better get you back."

I followed him out of the ward, down the corridors and

into the grey daylight. My stomach seized up. I felt sick. I felt heavy and stiff from my shoulders down to my feet. My chest tightened and I couldn't get my breath. I grabbed the wall before falling. Dave turned around and saw me. "Here," he said, and put his arm around my waist and helped me walk.

We sat in silence for the whole journey. There was nothing to say. Dave kept his eyes on the road in front. They were red and puffy. When we got back, he sat me down in the living room and covered me with a blanket. Marie came in and she shared a smile with Dave, then turned and smiled at me. She knew.

"Make him a tea, will you?" he said, and turned to leave.

Marie nodded. She turned to me and rubbed my arm, "Are you hungry?"

I shook my head, "Just tea, please."

A few days later, Dave came over to me after work and said, "I've got something to show you." He led me to his car and we drove through the town and stopped outside the supermarket, facing the door. He turned off the engine and looked at me.

"How old do you think I am?" he said.

"Fifty?" I said.

He laughed. "Almost sixty." He looked away from me and out of the windscreen towards the supermarket. It was a bright, sunny day and there were lots of people going in and out of the shop.

"Do you see that guy sat down there?" he said, not moving his eyes from the doorway. He pointed to the side of the supermarket, just past the trolleys. I looked and saw an old guy in dirty clothes. His jeans were too big for him and his coat was torn. He had a grey beard that was stained yellow-brown around his mouth from nicotine. He was drinking wine from the bottle and begging.

"How old do you think he is?"

I puffed out my cheeks. "Probably sixty," I said.

Dave raised his eyebrows and nodded, 'You'd think so, but he went to school with my son. He's thirty-eight."

"From drinking?" I said.

"Booze, fags, drugs. You name it."

We both sat looking at him for a few minutes in silence. The guy held his hand out when people walked past to get a trolley, but they didn't look at him. He was invisible to everyone but us. He pulled his legs up to his chest and held them with his arms. He lifted the bottle to his lips and drained it. As he looked around, his gaze stopped on us. Then he looked away. He took out a cigarette and lit it. He blew the smoke out and turned to us again and tilted his head. We looked at him and he looked at us. He knew we were staring at him. We kept looking and so did he.

Dave started the engine and pulled away. I kept my eyes on the guy, as we drove towards the exit. He was still watching. We drove out onto the road and he kept looking as we got to the end and turned the corner.

10

I sat straight up in bed, held my breath and stared into the black. The air was thick and hot. My legs and back were wet with sweat, sticking me to the sheets. I saw shapes writhing and twisting in the dark moving across my room, coming from the window. A cold shiver shook my back, shot down through my body and into my feet.

There was a presence in my room.

God, help me.

I breathed the shortest, quietest breaths I could. My body went rigid. I stared into the darkness, hoping to see nothing and relieve my fear. I could hear my heart beating faster and faster.

Thudthud thudthud thudthud thudthud thudthud.

"Leave me alone," I said, and waited. But nothing changed.

I shuffled my back against the wall and pulled the covers up around my neck. I didn't blink. I watched and watched the blackness.

Is there something there?

I stared for a while longer, until my eyelids became heavy and fell shut. I slipped down onto the bed and tried to sleep.

I hid my head under the covers, pushed my face into the pillow and tried to force sleep. As I lay there, I chanted.

There's nothing there, there's nothing there, there's nothing there.

But then, far off in the distance, I heard footsteps. A faint, slow thud of feet on the ground and the crunch of leaves and twigs beneath them. They were coming towards my room, getting closer and closer. Each step was louder and clearer. Again, I breathed shallow breaths that made no sound. My heart knocked in my chest. Then the steps stopped outside my window.

I froze, unable to breathe, and listened. It stayed quiet.

Maybe I imagined it. Maybe I dreamt it.

Then they started again, but this time they were getting quieter. They were heading away from my window.

This isn't real. It's just paranoia.

I listened and took shallow breaths, until they had gone.

I woke the next morning drenched in sweat and with intense palpitations that I could feel in my neck. Light streamed through the curtains and made me feel safe. I looked out onto the overgrown area behind the annex and everything looked normal. There were no footprints or any signs that someone had been there. It was green and calm. It made no sense.

I sat on the bed and sobbed. The same thing had been happening night after night for weeks and I'd not slept a full night through. I leant over and the muscles in my stomach tensed and hurt. I was heavy and numb. I lit a cigarette and smoked it in quick, deep drags. I lit another, inhaling the smoke as deep as I could get it. It helped me. It relaxed me. I took a long drink from a bottle of whisky and felt the warmth spread out from my stomach to the rest of my body. My chest was tight. My heart raced. I took another gulp.

I got back into bed and leant on the wall, sipping the whisky and smoking and trying to get my breath back.

Another gulp and the whisky was almost empty.

The pain in my stomach eased. My chest loosened. I

drained the last mouthful from the bottle and breathed. I felt better, but still tired from the disturbed sleep, so I let myself drift off.

A loud knock at my door woke me. "Where the hell have you been?" Lee said, opening the door.

I sat up and looked at him.

"You're on day shift and you're late."

I stood up and tried to pull on my work trousers, but fell back onto the bed. Lee came over and pulled me up. "You stink of booze," he said, and helped me put my shoes on. He pulled a T-shirt over my head and walked me down to the hostel. Usually when I did something stupid, Tracy said things like, *bless him, you can't stay mad with him can you? He's just so cheeky and lovable*, but that day I'd crossed a line.

As I walked in the door, I saw Dave stood there with his arms folded and his face red. Through clenched teeth he said, "What time do you call this? I've had to start the packed lunches for you."

"Sorry, I overslept," I said, and walked over to the counter to take over. I picked up the bread knife and dropped it. As I bent down to pick it up, I fell backwards onto the floor.

"Are you drunk?" Dave said, and came over to pull me up. He stood in front of me and put his face in mine and sniffed. He shook his head. "How dare you turn up in this state? You're useless like this."

I lowered my head and looked at the floor.

Then he shuffled around a bit, turned even redder and said, "And stop using the office computer for porn. I know it's you." Then he walked out and slammed the door.

I felt so sick, that I couldn't be near food. I shut myself in the office and lay on the floor with my cheek and stomach touching the cold tiles for relief, and tried to sleep. But it was no good. Every time I shut my eyes and tried to drift off, I thought of the footsteps behind my room and the black shapes in the dark. I needed a drink. There were no guests and no other staff, so I got up and went hunting for booze. In the self-catering kitchen, I found two bottles of beer and a bottle of gin with half left. Back in the main kitchen, I prepared breakfast. I had two of everything: bacon, sausages, hash browns, eggs, field mushrooms, buttered toast, all washed down with the two beers.

And a pint of gin and orange juice on the side.

Afterwards, I wondered around the creaky Victorian house snooping in the rooms. In the lounge, I sat on the leather chesterfield and drank gin from the bottle. I took chocolate from the tuck shop and ate it knocking balls around on the pool table in the games room. Then I went into the guest bedrooms. I walked into one of the single rooms, sat on the bed and looked out of the window. I could see the sea far off in the distance between the rooftops. I saw a small boat drifting across the bay heading for the other side. I watched as it made its way at its own pace. Slow and steady. It got to the cliff edge and slipped past a millimetre at a time, until it passed away out of sight.

I lay back on the bed and thought about sleep. How I wanted to drift into it with ease, until I was there without trying. As I got up to leave, I saw a brown medicine bottle on the bedside cabinet. I picked it up and read it, *amitriptyline, may cause drowsiness, do not drink alcohol.* I took a handful of the pink pills and put them in my pocket. I thought they'd probably get me to sleep or at least give me a buzz.

As soon as I finished at five, I tried the pills. In my room, I opened a bottle of wine, poured a large glass and swallowed four of them. I lit a cigarette and sat on the bed and waited. I finished the wine and a few cigarettes and couldn't feel anything, so I went and got another bottle. As I walked back from the kitchen, my legs were lead. The air around me was syrup. Behind my knees and in my hips painful aches formed and I longed to sit down.

I got back to my bed and flopped onto it. My eyes felt

dry, so I blinked and blinked. They closed, but when I pulled them open again it took effort and concentration. Each blink used more effort, so I pulled them open and poured myself more wine. I was glad they were working, but I wanted more. More drowsiness, more oblivion. I had no work for the next two days, so I could sleep for as long as my body wanted. I didn't have the strength to undress, so I kept my work clothes on and slipped under the covers. I looked down at the pills and counted at least another four. I threw them into the back of my throat and gulped the wine down with them, hoping they would take me off to a long and undisturbed sleep. I put a cigarette between my lips, but couldn't muster the strength to light it.

I hope I see nothing but darkness now.

I slipped down into the bed. My body was so heavy it was pinned down. My ears heard nothing but white noise. My consciousness reduced down down down down down. And was gone.

Darkness.

Darkness.

But then in that darkness came a dream. I saw myself in my room in bed. I got out of my bed in slow motion. I moved through the annex looking for something or someone, but I found nothing and no one. I was looking through the eyes of the dream version of me and everything was blurred. I tried to speak and it came out garbled like another language. Then the dream dissipated and everything went dark again.

Darkness.

Cold.

Oblivion.

I was in the dream again, but now the dreamscape was dark too. I walked through the dark and shapes came at me from all sides and banged into my body. I stretched out my arms and pulled the long objects away to propel me along. I had to lift my legs really high to stalk through whatever was entangling my legs. I pushed on, but it became thicker and harder to move. I let myself fall and sit. Then the darkness overcame me again and the dream stopped.

Dark and cold.

It's a dream. Just a dream. You're dreaming. I was in the dream again, but this time it was light and there were trees all around me. I looked down and I was wearing my work clothes and they were covered in mud and leaves and twigs.

It's only a dream, I thought. I got up and started to free myself from the undergrowth. I cut my hand on broken glass and held it up. I could see the blood glistening. There was no pain. I wiped it on my clothes. I spun around, but trees were the only thing I could see in every direction. I knew I had to get out, but didn't know the way. I set off in one direction and kept pushing through the branches and twigs and undergrowth, but it just kept getting thicker and harder until I was stuck from head to toe and couldn't move any further in that direction. So I pulled myself free and headed the opposite way. That way became clearer. I looked down at my arms and they were covered in scratches and cuts and my legs ached. I pushed on, and in the distance I saw a hut.

I need to get there and then I'll wake up. That's where I'm conscious.

I walked and it got closer and closer. But there was no door in the building, only windows. I headed to the biggest window I could see. I speeded up until I was stood right in front of it. I looked in with my hands cupped, but there were curtains pulled on the other side. I lifted my hand up and banged on the window. There was no answer. I banged again, but still no answer. I followed the bricks around past one corner then another trying to find the front of the building. When I found a door, I was stood in front of the annex.

Am I awake? Is this real?

I still felt heavy and my eyes were blurred and hazy, but I couldn't wake up.

I need to get back to bed in the dream and then I'll wake up.

I opened the door to the annex and went in. My room was where it was in reality, so I opened that door and went inside. I walked over to the bed and no one was in it, so I got in and closed my eyes and slept.

Darkness again.

Warmth and darkness.

Darkness.

Dark.

I woke sometime later. I was stiff and aching all over. I pulled back the covers and stood up to get a drink. I looked down at my clothes and they were covered in dirt and leaves, rips and tears. I looked at my hand and it was crusty with brown dried blood.

Every night I drank until I blacked out. In the middle of the night, I'd call my parents and wake them up. They knew I'd never remember what I'd said, but they spoke to me anyway.

One night, I called late and my mum answered.

"There's someone in my room," I said.

I heard her sigh. "Well, tell them to go to their own room," she said, her voice thick and weary. She waited for me to answer.

I took a deep breath and said, "It's not a person."

The line went quiet for a few seconds.

"Who is it, then?"

"I don't know. I can't see them, but I can feel them."

"Don't be silly."

"I can hear footsteps outside crunching the leaves, but when I look no one's there, then my back goes cold and I sweat and I can't sleep."

She went quiet again.

"It's just the drink playing tricks," she said. "Go back to bed."

"It's not, it's something evil."

She sighed again. "Andrew, it's late. Go to sleep and you'll feel better tomorrow." Then she hung up.

I wanted to tell her that I thought it was the devil coming to my room at night to take me to hell, but it sounded crazy.

I wanted to tell her that I felt sad and lonely and didn't want to be alive anymore. I wanted to tell her, but I couldn't.

It was my day off, and I'd woken up from a disturbed sleep. I was too tired to wash or clean my teeth, so I pulled on some clothes and went through to the kitchen for a drink. I couldn't focus my eyes or ears. Everything was fuzzy. There were too many thoughts in my head rushing around in and out of focus, but there was one that stayed at the forefront, *I can't take this anymore*.

Inside the fridge were four beers. I picked one up, opened it and drank it. I picked up another and drank it, gulping and gulping until it was gone and then burped out the gas. I took the other two and sat down in the living room. I lit a cigarette and pulled hard on it. The pressure was there in my chest suffocating me, but the cigarette helped. I pulled on it again and held it in. I sat cross-legged and tensed my stomach to try and rid it of a hollow, hungry feeling. I put my head in my hands and ground my teeth and squeezed my eyes shut. I couldn't get rid of the pain and tension. I hit my head with my hands and shouted. Nothing was working.

I lit another cigarette and smoked and smoked till it was gone. I downed another beer. The pressure in my chest tightened, the hollowness in my stomach got wider, and my legs were restless. I put my shoes on and headed out of the annex with the last beer. I walked past the hostel too fast for anyone to see me and headed down the hill looking at the ground. The tarmac was grey, the kerbstones were grey, the shadows all around me were grey. But I felt better walking. The movement gave me focus and released some tension. As I got to the bottom of the hill, I'd finished the beer and all I could think about was another drink, so I went into The Ship.

"Double vodka and coke," I said, and sat on a bar stool.

The bartender brought me my drink and went to serve an older guy who'd just come in.

"Hi Frank, what can I get you?"

"Pint of best and a packet of cheese and onion," he said, scratching his huge belly, "oh, and stick a pickled egg in the crisps, will you?"

The thought of the crisps and egg made me feel sick. I ran to the toilet and let out a torrent of vomit into the urinal. It was all liquid. I looked in the mirror and my eyes were bloodshot, watery, and surrounded by deep, dark rings. My cheeks were sallow and covered with small red veins. I looked old.

Back in my seat, I ordered another vodka and coke. I downed it and lit a cigarette. The fat guy was upending his crisp packet and shaking them into his mouth. They were falling onto his jumper and resting on his gut. He chewed with his mouth full and gulped his beer. He stood up, belched, and rubbed the crumbs off his jumper onto the floor.

Dirty git, I thought. Anger filled my stomach and chest.

I lifted my glass and caught the attention of the bartender. "Another," I said, and lit a cigarette.

"That everything?" he said, as he put my drink down.

I picked it up and downed it. "No, two more."

"Okay," he said, and smiled. "Having a bad day?"

I shrugged. "They're all bad."

He nodded. "Gimme a shout if you need anything."

It took me only a few minutes to finish the two drinks, and then I got up and left. I hated drinking in a public place with other people. I needed to be alone. Away from judgement. I decided to buy some booze and go back to the annex, so I headed to the supermarket.

Inside, I walked towards the booze aisle with a basket, but turned back and swapped it for a trolley. Once in the aisle with the gleaming bottles of multi coloured booze, my stomach felt light and jittery. My focus returned and I picked bottles up and read them. I chose half a dozen bottles of wine, a case of beer, a bottle of vodka, a bottle of bourbon, and some coke and lemonade.

It was overkill, but I didn't want to run out.

Back at the annex, I sat down on the armchair straight in front of the television and filled the coffee table in front of me with the booze. I had my cigarettes, an ashtray, and a corkscrew. I had no reason to move except for the toilet. I poured half a bottle of red wine into a pint glass and downed it. I refilled it and finished it in a few gulps. The pressure in my chest was still there and the hollowness in my stomach was back. I lit a cigarette and put on the TV. I stared at the screen, while I drank another bottle of wine.

Drew and Beccy walked through on their way to the kitchen. As Beccy passed, she gave me a scowl, but Drew stopped and said, "Having a party?"

I laughed. "Sort of. Wanna drink?"

Beccy raised her eyebrows and said, "No thanks," and continued into the kitchen.

"She's still annoyed you ate her sausage rolls," Drew said.

I shrugged and took another gulp of my wine.

"Are you coming to make dinner?" Beccy called through.

"Yes darling," he said, and raised his eyebrows.

I finished the wine and felt frustrated that I wasn't getting as drunk as I wanted. Or that the hollowness in my stomach was still there. I opened the bourbon and poured a glass. I lit a cigarette and took a drag. My chest was still tight. Nothing was working. I couldn't relax. I sped up. Gulp, drag, gulp, drag, gulp, drag until the warmth emanated from my stomach through my body. I glugged more bourbon into my glass and kept the rhythm going – gulp, drag, gulp, drag, gulp, drag – until I felt numb and fuzzy. It was getting on for five and Lee would be finished soon. I needed a drinking buddy. I gave up on the glass as the bourbon was nearing its last quarter, then sipped the rest from the bottle. The warmth of the spirit combining with the satisfying smoke of my cigarette, had done the job and I felt lighter. I sat back, stretched out and finished the bourbon.

The door to the annex flung open, and Lee said, "Dinner is served," as he carried over an oven dish filled with lasagne on his upturned palm.

I laughed. "Get it in the oven and get a drink," I said, gesturing to the table of booze.

"You look wasted already."

I shrugged. "Only half way there."

Lee dived into the vodka trying to catch up. He filled a pint glass with half vodka, half coke and it was gone in seconds. He made another.

"Down in one?" I said.

"You know me well." He tipped it back in one long gulp. "Been drinking all day?" he said.

I nodded and smiled.

I pushed Lee to drink several pints of vodka and coke and he was falling over trying to get the lasagne out of the oven. I opened a bottle of red to go with it.

I ate a few mouthfuls and stopped. "This is awful."

"Get it down you. Fussy git."

"I'll be sick," I said. "Here, have mine." I picked up a handful off the plate and threw it at him.

Lee jumped up as the mound of food rolled off his clothes onto the floor, leaving a red and brown stain. "Come here." He grabbed some off his plate and rubbed it into my hair.

I laughed and licked some off my face. "Needs more wine," I said, and poured a glass of wine over my head. It dripped down my face and off my chin.

We threw more food and wine until Lee looked as bad as me, then we slumped down out of breath.

"Fag?" I said.

And we lit our cigarettes and smoked and laughed.

"What the hell are you doing?" said Marie, as she walked in.

"Having dinner. Want some?" Lee said, and threw a handful of the cold lasagne at Marie.

"You're so gonna regret that." Marie dug her hand into the dish of pasta and pulled out a huge mound. Lee stood up and tried to back away, but she chased him and rubbed the lasagne into his hair and face.

"Some wine?" I said, and poured a full glass down the back of her neck. She shrieked and chased me across the room and threw some back at me, but I was already so covered that my white T-shirt looked tie-dyed.

"You can pour me a glass for that," Marie said, and slumped on the couch panting. "I've got a date tonight," she said, and laughed.

We got through another two bottles of wine between the three of us, before Marie went off to get a shower. Me and Lee had taken off our T-shirts and were sat bare-chested doing shots of vodka. I stood up to go to the toilet, and that's when I realised how drunk I was. I fell into the door and onto the floor, before dragging myself along the wall to get there.

When I got back, Lee said, "Let's call it a night."

"Lightweight," I said. "Let's finish the vodka." There was only a couple of inches of it left, so I poured out two more shots and we threw them back.

"Last one," Lee said. I poured the rest of the vodka out.

After downing it, I threw my glass behind me and it smashed on the wall. Lee laughed and threw his at the wall too. I opened a bottle of wine and made Lee stay and drink it with me. I filled our glasses and we drank.

"I'm off to bed," Lee said, and threw his glass at the wall again, but that time it shattered all over my back. I sat there and felt anger build in my stomach and start to rise up.

"Idiot," I said.

Lee laughed. "Just messing, chill out."

I stood up and stumbled over to him, "I'm not messing," I said, an inch from his face.

He pushed me and said, "Get to bed."

Then before I knew it, I'd pulled back my arm and flung my clenched fist into his face, breaking his glasses.

"What the hell?" Lee said, and put his hands to his head.

I froze. All the anger had gone and I didn't know why I'd hit him. "Lee," I said, and went to apologise.

"Leave me alone," he said, and went to his room and locked the door.

I slumped down in the chair and lit a cigarette.

What the hell were you thinking?

It was the only time I'd hit anyone. I always shied away from violence. I was the one who ran in the opposite direction. I never retaliated, even when I'd been hit. I'd been friends with Lee from the first day I got to Swanage. I got stoned with him, drunk with him, and made giant fry ups in the middle of the night with him. We were drinking partners, housemates, and colleagues. I had no reason to hit him.

You idiot. I hit myself in the temples.

I sat and tried to think it through, but couldn't figure out why I'd done it. I drank what was left on the table. I drained the dregs from the vodka and bourbon, drank a glass of wine and finished the remaining beers. I put my head in my hands and hit it saying, "Idiot, idiot, idiot," over and over again. I picked up a glass and threw it at the wall. I picked up a bottle and threw that at the wall.

"Idiot," I shouted, as loud as I could. I picked up all the bottles and threw them around the room, shattering them on the wall and covering it with splashes of red wine and whisky. I cried and threw myself down on the ground. I cut my hands in the glass as I fell, and hit my head on the table. I looked over at the wall where we'd been collecting our empty bottles on three big shelves. In the centre was a huge scrumpy bottle shaped like a demijohn. I walked over and pulled it down off the shelf. I looked it over, and then walked to the other side of the living room and threw it as hard as I could at the window. The glass shattered and the bottle crashed onto the path outside. I walked out of the room, into the garden and behind the annex. I hid in the darkness of the trees and bushes. I cried and shivered and beat my fists on the dirt and leaves, until I fell asleep.

I woke up at seven the next morning, just as everyone was going down to cook breakfast for the guests. I could hear them inside the annex getting ready to leave.

As the front door opened, I heard Drew say, "What happened last night?"

"Didn't you hear?" said Marie.

"Couldn't hear anything over Beccy's snoring."

"Andy hit Lee and smashed up the lounge."

Their voices trailed off and I stayed behind the annex leaning on the wall out of sight. I was still drunk and so scared that my heart was beating with a violent thudding that I could feel in my throat. I lit a cigarette and pulled hard. My mind flicked back to the moment I hit Lee, and a sharp pain shot across my temples. I stood up, my jaw wobbled and saliva pooled in my mouth. I put my hands on the wall and heaved. Hot, alcoholic vomit gushed out onto the brick and seeped down to the ground. I stayed in that position for a minute and my stomach tensed again and another slew of vomit splashed down the wall. My mouth was dry and I needed a drink, but I didn't want to bump into anyone, especially not Lee, so I waited. I was covered in dirt and had no top or shoes on. I shivered, but not just from the cold.

What is wrong with me?

I lit another cigarette. My hands shook. My legs shook. My lips shook. Hot tears ran down my cheeks onto my bare chest. I felt weak. I felt ill. I felt scared.

God, help me.

After I finished smoking, I wiped my eyes and stood up. The annex was quiet and I decided to go in and go to bed. I crept round the side and saw the broken window and smashed bottle on the path. It was all just as it was when I'd done it. My heart raced. My chest tightened. My stomach burned. I went in and through to the kitchen and opened the fridge. There was beer and an opened bottle of wine. Neither were mine, but I took the wine and gulped it down. I opened the beer and took a sip, then walked through to my room with it. I closed the door and locked it. I got into bed, curled up and faced the wall. I screwed my eyes shut and tried to think of nothing and no one and find oblivion in sleep. But sleep wouldn't come. I shook and cried. Thoughts filled my mind about Lee, about life, about the mess I caused with everything and everyone. I had to stop the thoughts. I got out of bed and rummaged through my things to see if I had any pills or weed left. Nothing. I went into the living room and into the kitchen to check for booze. Not a drop. Then I heard the gate to the garden open and saw Dave walking up the path. I went back into my room and got into bed, pretending to sleep.

He knocked on my door. "Andy, you in there?"

I took quiet, shallow breaths and stayed as still as I could.

"Andy?" He pushed the door open and stood there. "We need to talk. Come to the office at four, okay?"

I froze. My heartbeat was so loud I was sure he could hear it. There was no way out.

"Andy?"

I knew I had to face them, so I grunted, but stayed facing the wall.

"We'll see you later," he said, and closed the door.

I stared at the wall, shaking and crying. I made myself get up for a wash. After I got dressed, I ate some toast and decided that this was my last day in Swanage. They would send me home at the very least. I sat on my bed smoking and biting my nails until it was ten minutes to four, then I walked down to the office. Dave and Tracy were sat side by side facing an empty chair. I went into the room. No one else was there.

Tracy smiled as I came in, and I smiled back.

Dave didn't smile. "Sit," he said, and pointed at the chair.

I nodded and sat down. I looked down at my knees and the floor in front. I could feel my jaw going loose again and saliva pooling under my tongue, but I clenched my teeth and told myself I wasn't going to be sick.

"Tell us what happened last night?" Dave said.

I opened my mouth, but I was stuck on 'I'. My mind couldn't find the words and my mouth wouldn't work.

"It's okay, just tell us," Tracy said.

I looked at her and felt safe. There was no judgement in her eyes.

"I hit Lee," I said.

"Why?" said Dave.

I shook my head and kept shaking and shaking until tears fell down my cheeks.

"And the smashed window and bottles in the lounge?"

I nodded again.

Tracy got up and stood next to me and rubbed my shoulder. "Lee doesn't want the police involved," she said.

"But he wants to know it won't happen again," said Dave.

I shook my head. "It won't," I said.

"It'll go in the incident book and you'll have to pay for the damage."

I nodded.

They weren't sacking me, but I didn't feel any better. The emptiness in my stomach was there and nothing could fill it. We sat in silence for a minute. They both looked upset too, but I didn't know why.

Then Tracy said, "Can we help you?"

I looked and saw tears in her eyes. I shook my head and looked away, as I started to cry again.

"Tell us what we can do," she said, her voice breaking.

My chest heaved and I sobbed. I put my head between my knees. Tracy cried and Dave looked away.

"Stop me drinking," I said, "just stop me drinking."

11

It was August, and the heat woke me from a troubled sleep. My sheets were wet with sweat and so was the bed beneath me. The air in my room was thick and suffocating. I felt hollow. My tongue was dry and my throat full of phlegm. I went to the kitchen and drank two cans of beer and hacked up the mucus into the sink. Back in my room, I sat on the edge of the bed and tried to calm the shaking in my hands, but it seemed to spread to the rest of my body instead. I picked up a bottle of whisky from the side and took a few gulps. The hollow feeling in my stomach felt better and I breathed.

I breathed.

I lit a cigarette and smoked it in four or five deep drags, then used it to light another. I took that one slower with sips of the whisky. As my body calmed down and stopped shaking, I started to feel more comfortable. But my mind was teeming with thoughts.

Look at yourself.

You're a mess.

Everyone is sick of you.

All you do is hurt them.

I hit myself in the temples with my fists until they ached, saying, "Shut up, shut up, shut up." The thoughts died down into the background. I took a cold shower to shock myself. I brushed my teeth and threw up. There was blood. More blood than just from my gums, but I ignored it and swilled it away.

I pulled on my jeans and a T-shirt and headed out. I didn't want to see Lee. It was too awkward. I'd said sorry so many times it was beginning to annoy him more than the punch did. I walked with my head down and eyes squinted, trying to escape the sun. At the bottom of the hill, I was shocked by the amount of people milling around the streets. I went into The Ship to avoid them. I ordered a pint and lit a cigarette. I had to take it steady, though, as Marie had organised a party that afternoon and warned me not to turn up drunk. Her boyfriend and his friends would be there, as well as everyone from the hostel.

"Same again?" said the barman.

I looked down and I'd all but finished my pint. I nodded.

I walked to the toilet and as I passed the back door I saw that the beer garden was filled with people. Then when I got back to my seat, more people were coming into the pub and I had to leave. I had to get away. My chest was tight and the hairs on my neck prickled at the thought of someone speaking to me. The bartender was walking back over, so I stood up and looked at the change in my pocket. He walked over to someone else.

I have got to leave.

I went back out into the crowded street, put my head down and walked to the supermarket. I needed to get wine to take to the party. Inside, it was much quieter. I headed to the booze aisle and looked at all the bottles. But I couldn't decide what to get. Red, white, sparkling, it wasn't a big decision, but I stood there confused. I walked up the aisle looking at bottles going from black to red, then pink to yellow and green.

What do I get? What do I get?

I walked back down the aisle and picked up a few, but put them back. I started taking short, sharp breaths as my chest tightened and tightened.

I can't take this. I can't take it. I can't take it.

I hit my palms on my head and said, "Calm down, calm down, calm down." I sucked air in through my nose in big breaths, but my chest felt starved of oxygen. My lungs were squeezed and every breath I tried to get into them didn't make it. *I've got to get out of here*, I thought, but just stood there staring at the wine.

Get out, get out, get out, get out.

I clenched my fists and through my teeth I said, "Calm down. Just get some wine and go." I turned back to the bottles and they all merged into one strip of shining, blurred colour stretching out before me. I put my hands to my eyes and they were filled with tears. I took my T-shirt and pulled it up to my face and wiped them away, until I could see. I reached out and picked up a bottle that shone out from all the others. It had a mirrored finish. I put it up to my face to read and saw myself looking back. My face was distorted. It was long and drawn out. The skin was white, the eyes black holes with red rims. The mouth a stretched oval. The figure looked trapped inside the bottle. It was screaming for help and reaching out, but the glass encased it and held it in. It was trapped.

I felt trapped.

I was trapped.

I saw my hand slacken and the bottle roll down my palm. The white face with black eyes was still staring at me from inside the bottle as it fell. I watched as the bottle spun and the face spun, round and round and round, until it hit the floor and exploded into pieces. The wine splashed up my legs. The pieces of mirrored bottle spread out into the aisle before me. The face was gone. Broken into a thousand shards. My knees buckled, and I fell forward onto them in the glass and wine. I reached out and tried to clean the mess with my hands, scooping the debris up and pulling it towards myself and into a pile between my legs. Then the floor started swirling with red. Little twists of scarlet floating through the spilled wine and connecting the pieces of broken glass. There was no sound. I could hear nothing around me just the pump of blood in my head and the thud of my heart behind my ribs.

Thud thud thud thud thud thud thud thud thud thud

I looked up and two supermarket employees were walking up the aisle towards me, but each step took a minute. They mouthed words, but there was no sound. They put their hands up, showing their palms. I could just make out *it's okay* by reading their lips, as they got closer to me.

Thud thud thud thud thud thud thud thud thud thud

I looked down and tried to clean the glass again. I pulled the little fragments toward a pile before me. Streaks of red spread further out onto the ground again. The red lines pointed at me from every direction all around the floor, and all around me and the mess I was sat in. My chest was tight. So tight, I couldn't breathe. The blood became more rapid in my ears. I could hear the thud, feel the thud, taste the thud on the back of my tongue.

Thudthud thudthud thudthud thudthud thudthud

The two guys reached me and one put his hands on my shoulders. He pushed my arms down by my side and stopped me wiping up the glass. The other stood in front of me and mouthed, *Are you all right?* I looked at him, but my face felt numb. I parted my lips to speak, but words wouldn't come, so I shook my head and let my mouth hang open. He nodded and mouthed, *It'll be okay. We'll help you.* Then they pulled me up and put my arms around their shoulders and walked. I tried to walk, but my legs had no strength. I saw everyone stood at the checkouts staring at me. The staff stopped scanning the food, and stared. The customers stopped packing their bags, and stared. We went through a door and into a small room. They put me in a chair and wrapped a coat around me. I looked down at my hands and they were covered in blood. My clothes were covered in blood.

My whole body was shaking. My teeth chattered. My chest thudded.

Then I heard one of the guys say, "I'll get you a glass of water."

I nodded, and then looked down at my hands again. The blood was drying around shining splinters of glass poking out of my skin. I stared and stared.

"I've gotta go," I said.

He looked at me. His brow was winkled. "If you're sure," he said.

I could feel it in the bottom of my stomach waiting to bubble up again. If I focused on it the *thud thud thud thud* started in my ears and my chest squeezed all the air out. I pushed it down and held it back.

"I need to get back." I stood up. My legs were weak and shaking.

He nodded and smiled. "What about the wine?" He went out for a few minutes and returned with two of the mirrored bottles, shaking them in the air. I kept getting glimpses of my face in the bottles, as he held them for me. My stretched features flashing in and out of view. Me, still imprisoned. The blood pumped in my ears, in my chest, in my neck. My stomach contracted. I vomited on the floor.

"Sorry, sorry..." I said.

"Did you want different—"

"They're fine," I said, and steadied myself on the wall.

He put them through an unmanned checkout for me and put them in my arms. I took them and tried not to look at my reflection.

"Can I call anyone?"

I shook my head, thanked him and headed out. The streets were still packed. I put my head down and barged through the crowds and over the road, until I got to an alleyway that led up to the hostel away from the busy streets. I half walked half jogged up the hill, losing my breath, but it felt good to move. It took my mind off what was happening inside.

At the annex, I stood outside the front door and leaned on the wall to catch my breath. My hands were shaking. My legs were shaking. The blood pumped in my chest and neck. My stomach churned. I threw up over and over again on the grass, until I was empty. Then I dry heaved, making my throat sore. I went through to my room, changed my top and washed my hands. Then I sat in the lounge. I lit a cigarette and put the bottles on the table. I took a drag and blew it out in front of me, obscuring the mirrored surfaces. My jaw shook and my hand shook, but I kept smoking, hoping it would get better. I was sat in the chair in front of the TV, staring at the wall behind it. The sun was shining at the back of the annex, which left the lounge in shadow. I liked the cool air and darkness. It calmed me.

I picked up one of the bottles and looked again at my contorted face. It was as though I was looking at it under water, stretched and magnified. I didn't move. I stared and imagined that I was someone else looking at my lifeless face beneath the surface of the sea. My limp body floating and shifting in the current.

"They for the party? Marie said, walking through the living room. "I'll put them in the fridge." She reached out and took them, my trapped face leaving with her.

"I'm off to get some charcoal for the barbeque. Everyone's arriving in an hour," she said, twirling her car keys in her hand.

I tried to smile, but she knew something was wrong.

"You all right?" Marie said.

I nodded. She stood looking at me for a moment, then smiled and squeezed my shoulder.

I sat in that chair smoking and staring at the wall until people started to arrive for the party. I looked out of the window and saw a group of strangers talking and laughing with Marie, as she was cooking on the barbeque. I felt scared. Not scared of them, but of being with people. I thought they'd be able to see something wrong with me. That my face would give it away. I didn't want to see anyone, so I went into my room and sat on the bed. As I walked, I shook and felt unsteady on my feet. My legs were shaking so much that my teeth chattered. I needed a drink, but there was nothing in my room. I had to go outside. I clenched my fists, stood up and walked as steadily as I could through the annex and out into the garden.

As soon as I got outside, Marie said, "Andy, come and join us." So I walked over to her and her friends. She put a glass of wine in my hand and started introducing me to people. I smiled and looked at their laughing heads as she reeled off four or five names, but I didn't listen to any of them. I watched the half empty bottle of wine in her hand, waiting to see where she was going to put it.

I'd downed the wine and was stood there still shaking, my eyes following the bottle in her hands. One of her friends noticed and said, "Top him up, Marie. He looks parched."

Marie looked at me with narrowed eyes and poured me another glass. She laughed and told them I liked a good drink. They started chatting about people I didn't know, so I slipped off to find more booze.

There was a table filled with drinks people had brought, so I drained my glass and headed over to it. I looked for the strongest thing there and found a bottle of port. I poured a glass and drank it. Then I looked around, saw that everyone was busy in conversation, and took the rest to a quiet corner. I sat against the wall at the far end of the garden and poured another glass. But nothing felt right. I struggled to drink any more. I pulled my knees up to my chin and held my legs. My sight became blurred and I could hear nothing but my heartbeat.

Thud thud   thud thud   thud thud   thud thud   thud thud

Marie's boyfriend came and sat beside me and asked me what was wrong.

"What do you mean?" I said.

"You're sat on the ground crying."

I touched my face and felt the tears. I shrugged. "I don't know how to be happy."

He crouched down next to me. "I had a friend who went through something similar," he said, and took a drag of his cigarette. "He came around in the end. Talk to people. You'll feel better." He squeezed my shoulder and left.

I was wrung out. There were no words to speak. All I could think was, *I'm going to die, this is the end for me.* I finished the bottle of port, just to stop the shaking, and went into the annex. I heard a couple of people call my name, but ignored them. I went into the shower and turned it on. All I could hear was the water hitting the curtain. I got down onto the base of the shower and sat cross-legged under the flow of water, and closed my eyes. I let it beat down on my head and soak through my jeans and T-shirt. I listened to the drumming of the water and nothing else. I tried to think of nothing except the water and the sound it made.

I felt my body heave and weep. I wished I could die, but didn't have it in me to kill myself. I sat and sat in the flowing water, but felt no cleaner or better. I got out of the shower and went to my room. I took off my clothes, turned out the light, and got into bed. I didn't know what else to do or where else to go. Bed was my last refuge. I faced the wall and curled up. I squeezed my eyes shut and hoped I'd fade away. That I'd sink into the black oblivion and never wake up. That I'd disappear into the vastness of the universe. That I'd evaporate and float into the sky. I saw the dark behind my eyes and tried to lose myself in it and push into unconsciousness.

God, I don't ever want to wake up again.

I let go and fell into the darkness.

I saw a warm glow behind my eyelids. Red and yellow seeping through the black. I didn't move. The position of my body was just as it was the night before. The sound of static filled my ears and then the *thud thud   thud thud   thud thud   thud thud* of the blood.

I felt the shaking start across my back, between the shoulder blades and down into my thighs. It was a cold, sharp shaking. The bedcovers were tight in my fists. I held onto them and squeezed.

A gaping hollowness opened in my stomach and made me weak. I tensed and held it. Tensed and held it. But it wouldn't go.

Then the heat came. Beads of sweat tickled their way off my forehead into the pillow. My legs were wet and slippery against each other. I pushed the covers between them.

I dug in and stayed as still as possible.

Let me drift away.

> *Drift away.*
>> *Drift away.*

A knock. Two knocks. Three knocks and the slide of door on carpet.

A voice. "Andy, are you okay? Are you ill?"

Silence. Stillness.

I dug in. held on. Pushed into the bed.

> Dug in. Held on.

Drifted away.

Darkness again. Around me and behind my eyelids. I let my body roll over and face up. I opened my eyes one millimetre a second. I felt my heart thud. The dark was comforting. I saw the square of the ceiling and it looked smaller than the floor. It got smaller as I looked. Smaller and smaller and higher and higher. My chest tightened. I squeezed my eyes shut and pulled the covers over my head.

Voices were in my head. In the wall. I put my hands over my ears. But it was my name they were saying.

"Andy, Andy, Andy."

A presence in my room. The crunch of carpet fibres. The flop of clothes being dropped.

A hand touched me. My shoulder flinched.

"Mate, you're meant to be working."

Lee. It's Lee.

I pulled the covers over my head and pushed my face into the pillow.

I breathed hollow fibre.

Silence.

Heat filled the room. Filled my mouth. Filled my nostrils. My tongue was paper. My swallow dry.

I opened my eyes and looked around. There was a glass of water on the bedside table. I pulled myself up and drank.
Fell back into bed.

I felt the light drain from behind the curtains. The *wah wah wah* of the TV through the wall stopped, and the place became silent again.

Still and silent.

The crunch of leaves, one step at a time. My back froze. I tensed.

Then I let go.

I don't care anymore. I can't care.

The thudding in my neck made it difficult to swallow.

153

I breathed short and sharp.

Short and sharp.

God, help me.

Dave and Tracy were sat next to one another at the side of the bed. I watched them talk. I watched them watching me lying there.

"Can we help?" they said.

I didn't reply. I looked at their faces and then at the floor. I closed my eyes again and let go.

I drifted in the dark. I floated and drifted.

Floated and drifted.

Hold on. Hold tight. Hold on.

It was light again. I stood up on stiff legs and stilt-walked a few paces to the sink. I faced the mirror. My head rocked from side to side and back and forth. A fizzing sound sat low in my ears.

My stomach tensed and I opened my mouth for the vomit.

Heave.

Heave.

Heave.

I tried to catch my breath.

The mirror shook and I stumbled backwards. I found the bed and crawled in.

On the shelf at the bottom of my bed stood a bottle of vodka. I'd seen it and it had seen me. I reached out and took it. On the edge of the bed, I sat and looked down at it.

The scrape of metal on glass, as I turned the lid and removed it.

Thud thud, thud thud, thud thud.

My nose met the smell. Acrid, chemical, caustic.

Wobbling jaw.

I tilted it back and into my mouth. Then I let it dribble out and down my chest.

Again, I tipped it up and took a sip, but before it reached the back of my tongue I had to spit it out.

I took a cigarette out of my pack, rested it between my lips and flicked the lighter. I pulled the smoke into my mouth. I took a quick breath into my lungs and the smoke filled them. It stabbed my lungs.

My chest tightened.

I stubbed it out.

I got back in bed and stared at the wall.

It was dark.

It was light.

A sandwich lay on a plate on my bedside cabinet.

A cup of tea sat undisturbed. A skin forming on its surface.

It was dark.

My body ached. I couldn't lift myself up. I took a look around the room. Sink, wardrobe, bookcase, bedside table, bed, me. I closed my eyes. I tensed my body, then let go.

I felt the release. I felt the drift.

God, I want to float away.

I thought of the boat I saw sailing on the horizon down at Swanage bay when I first got there. I imagined being the boat. I felt the rocking movement of the water. The steady pull of the wind in the sails. The cut and slide through the waves. In the distance was water and sky going on and on forever. The beach receded behind and I headed out into nothing. I rocked and floated and moved into the distance, until I was a speck.

If you're there God, let me die.

Let me die.

Let me float away and vanish.

Let me die.

But what then?
   Where would I go?
   I was silent, still, semi-conscious, but this thought tugged at me. Pulled me back from the edge. Held me away from oblivion.
                            Let me go. Let me drift away.
   I pushed my face further into the pillow.

Where would I go?

I don't know.

But I'm not happy here.

My mind flicked back through the memories of schools, jobs, friends, but found nothing that brought me happiness. My family seemed far away, distant, unreachable. I had to stretch to find the memories. Deaths, arguments, distress came flooding back, but I kept reaching further and further.
   My chest thudded, as I rummaged through the past.
   I saw the house I grew up in and the small bedroom above the lounge where I slept.
   The hum of prayer filled my ears.
   Then there was peace, stillness, security, and warmth. I remembered the times I lay in bed and listened to those prayers beneath me, as I drifted off to sleep.
   Where had it all gone wrong?
   What was it Michael had said that night I overdosed and couldn't speak?

"Don't forget, he's always there for you, wherever you go."
But where is he now?
> *Where are you, God?*
> *Where are you?*
> *Where are you?*

That breath I took after my mother sucked vomit from my airways.

That moment in Texas, at the chapel, in front of the cross.

That hand on my back when Michael was there.

Those two strangers who picked me up off Lee Lane on that dark night.

That morning I woke up after the yellow pills.

The way back, after I got lost on amitriptyline.

The care from Dave and Tracy when they tried to help.

The two guys in the supermarket.

This moment right now.

Was that you?
Is this you?

God, I need you right now.
> *Please help me. I don't want to die.*

My face was hot and wet and stuck to the pillow. The air was still. There was silence. I listened but heard nothing except the fizz of static in my ears.

God help me.

Silence. Stillness.

I lifted my face from the pillow and said, "God, I believe you're real. Please come and help me. Change me. Change my life. Change my attitude, change my feelings, change everything."

The thuds in my chest became stronger and faster. The hairs on my neck and arms and legs raised and tingled.

Then my chest loosened, and I breathed a deep breath.

I breathed and breathed deep breaths.

I was lying face down into the pillow. I raised my voice and shouted into it. "God, please fix the mess I've made."

Thudthud thudthud thudthud thudthud thudthud

Heat filled my body. Soft, warm, secure. I was floating in a bath of hot water. I turned over and lolled in the heat. There was a presence in my room. A presence that filled it. A presence all around me that passed through my body. It was heat, it was light, it was strength, it was power. It was new and it was real.

I opened my mouth and said, "Thank you. Thank you. Thank you."

The presence was electricity, flowing through every atom of my being and every particle of the room. My eyes were shut. I daren't open them. I squeezed them tighter and tighter, as lightning flashed through the air above me and lit the room an incandescent white. My eyelids became red and almost translucent. I couldn't open them.

Thudthud thudthud thudthud thudthud thudthud

The lightning shot into my body and through every vein, artery and vessel replacing the blood with white-hot energy. My neck arched back and the energy flowed from my head down through my body and out of my feet, pulling the pain and weakness away.

I felt a weight on my chest. It was hot and heavy and pressed me into the bed. The blinding light got brighter and brighter. I squeezed my eyes tighter and tighter but couldn't move my face away. I was pushed through the bed, through the floor, through the earth, through time, through everything.

The thuds in my chest became a snare drum.

Thudthudthudthudthudthudthudthudthudthud

Then the pressure released, and I was weightless. I floated in a sea of static. I tingled in every hair and every skin cell. I took a breath that filled my lungs, then released it. My lungs felt huge. I sucked air in and back out. In, then out. In, then out. In, then out.

My chest was a sail filled with wind.

I breathed.

I breathed.

I breathed.

"Thank you, God."

"Thank you."

I moved my hands. Then my feet. My arms. My legs. I was still there. I was still alive. Even more alive. The hollowness in my stomach was gone. My muscles were unclenched. I was relaxed. My body felt strong. My body felt new. My body felt healthy. I lifted my hands to my eyes and face, they were soaked in tears. There was no shaking, just tingling. A fizz of energy on my skin. A buzz in my stomach. My chest had no tightness, it was loose and free to breathe. My head was light. My mind free of thoughts. I felt alive. I felt new.

The glow of light started to fade in the room, but the warmth and comfort remained. The room fell still, silent, and dark. I didn't move or speak. I opened my eyes and it was dark. It was the middle of the night. The extreme heat and electricity had subsided and the beat in my chest had a new rhythm.

Thump thump   thump thump   thump thump   thump thump

The room was now back to normal. No bright lights. No electricity. No presence that filled it. But something had changed in me. I lay back on the pillow and smiled.

I breathed and relaxed.

Breathed and relaxed.

Breathed and relaxed.

Breathed.

12

I woke to an unusual sound coming from outside my window. A medley of tweets and taps. I walked over and pulled back the curtain. Two birds were walking along the ledge squawking at each other. They communicated with judders and tilts of their heads, then flew up into one of the trees together. I followed them as they flitted from branch to branch. Then watched as they ducked under and over green leaves that the sun was peeking through. I leaned on the inner ledge and looked from the overgrown bushes under the trees to the canopy of leaves up above. Everything was vivid greens and soft browns. The sun was high and bright and pushed its rays through gaps in the leaves, creating poles of light that focused in on small patches of ground.

I pulled myself away, brushed my teeth, took a shower and dressed. I was hungry and there was no food in the annex, so I had to go to the hostel. As I sat on the edge of the bed to put my shoes on, I saw the bottle of vodka on the shelf. The thuds started in my chest as I looked at it.

Thud thud   thud thud   thud thud   thud thud   thud thud
You don't need it. You don't need it.

I picked it up and unscrewed it. The smell turned my

stomach and I pulled it away. I swilled the liquid around and watched it cling to the inside of the bottle. I walked over to the sink and poured it away. The thuds in my chest slowed with each glug until the last drop.

Outside, I stood in the garden and squinted as I got used to the sun. I let it warm me and then basked in it for a few minutes. There were sounds I'd not heard before. The rustle of leaves in the breeze, the landing and taking off of birds on the wooden fence, the squawk of gulls on the highest point of the hostel roof. I turned around and took in as much as I could. The air was soft and sweet, and I could smell the grass and the trees in it. Further off, was the brine of the sea.

I lit a cigarette and the smell of smoke filled the air around me. The smoke was hot and caught in the back of my throat. It made me cough, but I carried on until stepping on it half way through. I headed down the path and towards the kitchen door. I stopped a few feet away and watched through the large window as Tracy, Lee, Marie, Drew and Beccy prepared food for the guests.

What should I say? How can I explain what's happened?

They were so busy, no one noticed me stood there. As I stared, I saw my face reflected in the glass. I looked younger, fresher. My cheeks had colour, my eyes were bright and my face was relaxed.

Will they recognise me?

I was still staring at myself, as the door swung open and Tracy stuck her head out. "Everything okay? How are you feeling?"

"Hungry," I said, and smiled.

She came outside, stood in front of me and looked at me. Her mouth was open and brow wrinkled.

I raised my eyebrows. "I'm fine," I said.

She smiled at me. "Come into the office."

I followed her through the kitchen and everyone looked at me. As I passed them they smiled, but said nothing.

Tracy and I sat in chairs facing one another and she said,

"Did you just wake up feeling better?"

"Kind of. I prayed last night and it helped. It helped a lot."

She laughed and scratched the side of her head, "Right. Okay, well that's great."

"When should I start work?"

She put her hands up. "There's no rush, you've been ill."

"But I want to get back to it." I said.

She leant back in her chair and looked outside. "Do you fancy doing a bit of gardening? We could do with tidying up a few areas."

"I'll start right now," I said.

She looked out of the window and up towards the pathway. "Behind the annex is long overdue."

I took saws, loppers, secateurs, and an axe to the back of the annex to clear the overgrown trees and bushes. I went to my room and put on some old clothes. As I walked through the hallway, I saw the phone and thought, *I'll call mum and tell her what's happened.*

"Mum, I spoke to God last night and I've changed."

It went quiet.

"What do you think?"

"I think it's far too early to be drinking."

I laughed. "I've not been drinking. I'm different."

She sighed, "I've heard it all before and I'm not interested. I'm going now, I've got to be at work," and she put the phone down.

I took my tools and headed behind the annex. It was so dense that I had to cut a pathway to get in. Inside, between the trees, it was cool. But the air was stagnant and close. The sun was barely getting through. All noise from outside was stifled by the undergrowth. It was like another world. I set to work clearing the area. My arms ached, as I hacked through the undergrowth and yanked it out into a pile. I cut down branches and trimmed bushes behind the bedrooms, creating an area big enough to sit out and enjoy the greenery. I walked down to my bedroom window and looked in. Everything was as I left it.

Once the area was cleared beneath, I cut down the higher branches that overhung it and the light flooded in. The colours became more vibrant and the wet, earthy, dense smell lightened and became greener and fresher. I sat down for a rest and watched the birds flying from tree to tree.

After working, I headed down into Swanage to avoid seeing Marie and everyone else. I didn't want to have to explain to them what had happened. All I had on my mind was making sure my mum believed me. As I walked along the high street the answer stood before me: flowers. I'd never bought her flowers before, but I knew what she liked. I looked through the options and chose sun-yellow roses arranged into a round bouquet. I ordered it to be delivered to her and on the card I wrote, *I love you. Andy.*

She'll believe me now. She has to.

Outside, it was hot and bright. I couldn't feel my heart beating or hear thoughts rushing through my mind. There was nothing I had to do and nowhere I needed to be. I wandered through the streets and looked in a few shops. I ate an ice cream and bought a pair of sunglasses.

But then I saw The Ship across the road, and the *thud thud thud thud thud thud* started in my chest, and my breathing became strained. I stopped on the pavement and stared at it. People behind me sighed and walked around, as I stood looking at the pub. My legs became weak and a bitter taste spread across the back of my tongue. I could hear buzzing in my ears and it seemed like everything had slowed down around me.

I walked across the street in a daze, my feet making no sound, and went in.

"Pint of best," I said.

"Sure," the barman said, "lovely day, eh?"

I pulled myself onto a stool. Then smiled and nodded, as he put a glass under the pump. I got a cigarette out and lit it. I took a long drag and as the smoke hit the back of my throat, I coughed.

"Sounds like you need this." He placed the beer in front of me and I stared at it. I looked into the dark brown liquid and watched the bubbles swirl around and settle. I could already taste the beer in my mouth. I put my hand around the glass, felt the condensation and lifted it towards my mouth. The blood pumped in my ears, neck and chest.

Thud thud   thud thud   thud thudt   hud thud   thud thud

The sounds of the pub became muffled and the shapes of the bar became blurred. Everything around me was blurred. Everything except my hand and the pint of beer. I lifted it further and it touched my lips. I tipped it and took a mouthful and returned the glass to the bar. I swallowed and my body froze. The cold beer flushing into my stomach made me shiver. My head felt hot and my back cold.

Thud thud   thud thud   thud thud   thud thud   thud thud

A voice said, *down it and get another, you'll feel so much better.* But another voice said, *leave the drink, leave the cigarette and get out now.*

I stared at the smoke twisting up from the end of my cigarette and the beads of condensation snaking down the glass.

Drink it.

Get out.

Thudthud thudthud thudthud thudthud thudthud

"You okay?" the barman said.

I looked up, and the sound of the pub came rushing back at full volume. The clink of glasses, the murmur of conversation, the thud of the door and people's footsteps. The blurred shapes regained their distinction and I saw everything as it was.

"Just remembered I need to be somewhere." I stood up, stubbed the cigarette out, pushed the beer away, and walked out into the warmth. I walked back across the road and set off towards the other end of town, where the coastal path led up to the top of the cliff. The thuds in my chest subsided and I breathed deep breaths. In the sun, I felt calm again. To my left, was the sea stretching out across the bay and towards the sun. I walked along its edge, until I came to the road that led to the pier. Along the sea's edge were boats rocking and bobbing on the water. I kept walking until I came to where the concrete pathway finished and the wooden boards of the pier started. They were thick and sturdy, but there were gaps between them. I stood and looked down through the boards. The inch-wide gaps were big enough to see the dark blue water shifting beneath. My legs went weak at the sight and I felt faint. I grabbed onto the railings at the side and caught my breath. A cool breeze blew across my face and I felt better. I stepped onto the boards, keeping a firm grip on the railings at the side. I took one step at a time and avoided looking down through the gaps. I kept my eyes on the end of the pier and the view out onto the sea and sky. I moved my hands up the railings with each step.

I took a deep breath and let myself feel my heartbeat. *Thump thump, thump thump, thump thump, thump thump, thump thump.* The faint sound of splashing came from below where the water slapped against the wooden posts. I kept pushing on.

As I made my way, I saw couples sitting on the benches in the centre of the walkway and families talking and laughing, as they walked back down the pier to the shore. I thought about my parents and imagined bringing them out onto the pier. We'd walk together and talk and laugh. As I reached the end, I made my way into the centre and stood holding the railings with both hands and looked down at the dark water. It was almost black. I stared and saw movements and shapes on the water's surface, revealing the currents beneath. I felt my stomach tense and my chest tighten.

I looked up to the horizon, the separation between sea

165

and sky. Then above at the vapour trails left by aircraft. Then further above them, to the sun. I felt the warmth on my face and the cool wind on my back. I closed my eyes, took a deep breath through my nose, and breathed out of my mouth.

In, then out.

In, then out.

In, then out.

I stood up straight, opened my eyes, and let go of the railings. I turned around and walked back down the pier to the shore.

Printed in Great Britain
by Amazon